Chronology of Communication
in the United States

ALSO BY RUSSELL O. WRIGHT
AND FROM McFARLAND

―――――――――――――

Chronology of Transportation in the United States (2004)

Chronology of Energy in the United States (2003)

Chronology of Labor in the United States (2003)

Chronology of the Stock Market (2002)

*Dominating the Diamond: The 19
Baseball Teams with the Most Dominant
Single Seasons, 1901–2000* (2002)

*A Tale of Two Leagues: How Baseball
Changed as the Rules, Ball, Franchises, Stadiums
and Players Changed, 1900–1998* (1999)

*Crossing the Plate: The Upswing
in Runs Scored by Major League
Teams, 1993 to 1997* (1998)

*Life and Death in the United States:
Statistics on Life Expectancies, Diseases
and Death Rates for the Twentieth Century* (1997)

*The Best of Teams, the Worst
of Teams: A Major League Baseball
Statistical Reference, 1903 through 1994* (1995)

*Presidential Elections in the United States:
A Statistical History, 1860–1992* (1995)

*The Evolution of Baseball: A History
of the Major Leagues in Graphs,
1903–1989* (1992)

Chronology of Communication in the United States

RUSSELL O. WRIGHT

McFarland & Company, Inc., Publishers
Jefferson, North Carolina, and London

Library of Congress Cataloguing-in-Publication Data

Wright, Russell O.
    Chronology of communication in the United States /
Russell O. Wright.
        p.   cm.
    Includes bibliographical references and index.

    ISBN 0-7864-2019-7 (softcover : 50# alkaline paper) ∞

    1. Communication — United States — History —
Chronology.   I. Title.
P92.U5W75   2004
302.2'0973 — dc22   2004022966

British Library cataloguing data are available

On the cover ©2004 Photospin

Manufactured in the United States of America

McFarland & Company, Inc., Publishers
  Box 611, Jefferson, North Carolina 28640
  www.mcfarlandpub.com

To Francis Granville Wright

ACKNOWLEDGMENTS

The series of U.S. historical chronologies that I am embarked upon (see page ii) continues to be truly a family enterprise. My wife, Halina, and my daughter, Terry Ann Wright, once again made invaluable contributions. Halina greatly aided the research process by collecting material from the Internet, our local library, and the *Los Angeles Times*. She also acted as a careful editor, and helped me recall geographical and mathematical data from our college days when it was needed to provide background material for the book.

Terry continued to demonstrate her mastery of Microsoft Word to an extent that would astound even Bill Gates. She created the figures in the Appendix, arranged and organized the text and its associated disks, and printed the manuscript in the required final format. She also made the Internet yield its trove of research material, and found ways to acquire research books for little more than the cost of shipping. She also kept me focused on creating the book by figuring out how to keep my personal files in order while observing my passionate need to maintain and classify every piece of paper I have ever received in my life.

I also want to acknowledge the contributions of my sons, Dan and Brian, who keep us all supplied with the latest in personal computers and peripherals, and who hold our hands to help us through the great crises that arise when, in our view, any of these technical marvels misbehave. In a real sense, the manuscripts for these books are produced by the Wright writing company.

CONTENTS

INTRODUCTION

If communication is the process of providing information to another member of the same species, then every creature on earth communicates, from the trail of ants on the ground to the huge whales in the sea. Communication is part of being alive, and the necessary instincts and skills are inborn.

In this chronology, discussion is confined to communication that takes place within the human species, beginning with the sort of communication that is unique to mankind: language and writing. Other forms of human communication are also considered, including pictures, various types of signals, musical sounds, and ultimately their simultaneous use on television, the Internet, and other modes of communication made possible by advancing technology.

Since this is a chronology of communication in the United States, there is a focus on what I call communication at a distance. This is because when settlers arrived in the United States starting in the 1600s, those settlers brought with them developed language and writing skills, books, knowledge of newspapers, and other methods of direct communication (flag and smoke signals, carrier pigeons, etc.). In the United States, since those early days, the development of communication has primarily involved electric and electronic methods so that we can enjoy instant communication with other people at great distances, both individually and en masse (e.g., via television, movies, and videos).

Communication Before Electricity

The beginnings of human communication through language are lost in the mists of time. Scientists believe that people have been communicating by writing for about 6500 years at the most, a trifling amount of time compared to the time people have been communicating via spoken languages. There are between three and four thousand identifiable languages that are or have been used. Today the most common languages are those that predominate in the most populous countries. Mandarin Chinese is spoken by 874 million people, and Hindi as used in India is spoken by 366 million people. English is probably the third most common, with 341 million speakers, although the number speaking Spanish is estimated to be just below English in some references (and in others, just ahead).

In terms of speakers in different countries around the world, English is far and away the closest thing we have to an international language. People in 104 countries speak English. French is next with 53 countries, but only 77 million total speakers. Spanish claims 43 countries, with between 322 and 358 million speakers. All other languages rank well behind in number of countries, and only nine individual languages have over 100 million total speakers. But if one were to add up all the countries where some form of Arabic is spoken, the number of countries would exceed 80 and the total number of speakers would be near 200 million.

English will probably continue to gain as an "international" language due to the technological leadership of the United States (English is the specified language used between airplanes and airport control towers around the world, for example), not to mention the great popularity of movies, videos, and music produced in the United States. This means more and more people will find it worthwhile to learn English as a second language.

Writing is believed to have developed no earlier than around 4500 B.C. in either Upper Egypt or ancient Mesopotamia (Sumeria — about where Iraq is located today), or it may have started nearly simultaneously in the two places. In Egypt writing took the form of hieroglyphics written on strips of the papyrus reed, while the Sumerians in Mesopotamia used clay tablets to record figures known as cuneiform writing. Progressing from pictures to a written language in a picture format is a logical step. Then alphabets were developed to try to capture the sounds of a given language, and written words began to appear. Writing also developed over time in most other countries of the world, but early efforts in China and among the Maya in Central America appear not to have started until about 1500 B.C. at the earliest.

The Egyptians learned to make and use ink to write on their papyrus, and so they could roll up the papyrus into scrolls, which were much easier to carry and to store than were the clay tablets of Mesopotamia. From these scrolls, the earliest libraries were created. One of the key uses of writing was to preserve the stories of the past to help educate future generations. We will return to this theme often in this chronology. The apparently incredibly rapid progress of technology and science in the last few hundred years compared to the thousands of years of written history that went before is largely due to the existence of books and libraries from which prior knowledge could be drawn. Each generation started a little further ahead of prior generations because the written accumulation of knowledge grew geometrically, until the rapid progress of today measures substantial change in years and decades, not centuries.

Most of the early libraries were eventually destroyed by various conquerors, and in the West and especially in Europe civilization fell into what many call the "Dark Ages." This is an obsolete term, for the Catholic Church and its monks were keeping the practice of reading and writing alive, although for about the first 1000 years after Christ hardly anyone else in Europe could read or write. The monks wrote on parchment, developed late in the time of the Roman Empire and made from the hides of sheep. After the wool had been removed, the skin was split into sheets (this took a lot of experience to do properly). Then the sheets were soaked for several days in lime, to remove the basic oils and decaying flesh, leaving just the tough fibers. After a thorough washing, each sheet was stretched on a frame to dry. Then it was turned into parchment by being scraped to an even thickness, dusted with chalk, and rubbed smooth with pumice stone. Vellum, a softer and even more expensive material, was made from antelope hides.

The advantage of these materials was that they would last almost indefinitely, as long as they were kept in a well-ventilated place, free from mice, bookworms, and tiny beetles. The materials took ink very well, but if the scribe made a mistake, he had to correct it by scraping away the surface with a knife and then repolishing the scraped place before making the correction. It was primarily by use of parchment that the monks of the Catholic Church kept alive the practice of writing during the so-called Dark Ages.

Writing on parchment with a pen led to changes in the form of written language: it was much easier to make simpler, smaller and more rounded letters instead of the previously used formal letters and "dignified" capitals. The education of children in the tenets of the Church also continued under the direction of the monks during this time. Books, however, were rare and very expensive, as they had to be laboriously copied by hand. Printing of books on what we now know as paper was taking place in China and Korea, although it is not clear if Europeans knew of this practice at the time. One basic problem with making books one copy at a time is that a Bible with 985 pages of text would have about 800,000 words, composed of approximately 4 million letters. Not only would great numbers of sheep be needed for the parchment, but obviously errors in copying one book from another would be likely to occur.

The solution to this problem appeared in the fifteenth century, with the development of moveable type cast in molds. The credit for this invention usually goes to Johann Gutenberg, a printer in Mainz, Germany. Many people think Gutenberg invented the printing press per se, but this is inaccurate. The Chinese and Koreans, as noted above, had been using printing presses and movable type long before Gutenberg. Many people in Europe were experimenting with printing presses and movable type at the time of Gutenberg, and even today some people credit Laurens Koster of Holland or Pamfilo Castaldi of Italy instead of Gutenberg with the key invention. But the story of Gutenberg has come down to us in great detail, and thus we'll give the honors to him, although he personally did not benefit greatly from his invention. As is the case with many inventors even in later years, business details involved in the financing of his invention kept Gutenberg from realizing any great riches.

In the 1430s, the Catholic Church decided to standardize its liturgy. Different countries used different versions. The church used Latin as its universal language, so once a standard version was agreed upon, that standard version would be used everywhere. But thousands of copies were required, and doing them by hand would take a long time, and inevitable errors would creep in. This would ruin the attempt to get a standard liturgy. Gutenberg saw an opportunity to create identical copies of the original, both quickly and at a low cost. The income from these books would produce the personal fortune he had set his mind on.

The key to low-cost printing of many copies of books was producing low-cost versions of thousands of pieces of movable type that were identical, durable, and capable of being used over and over. Printing even with movable type was not necessarily cheap if each piece of type had to be hand made in some fashion. What Gutenberg is credited with inventing (traditionally in 1437) was a hand mold about the size of a small matchbox. This mold held a die produced from a master punch. When the proper type of molten metal was poured into the mold, it took only a few seconds to produce a piece of type. All pieces of type formed this way would be identical, and a good type caster could make as many as four pieces a minute, or over 2,000 per day. Each piece was thus very inexpensive, and as many as were needed could be put into printing plates to produce the pages of the book. Then printing as many copies of each page as were needed for the total number of books desired would be relatively inexpensive on a per-copy basis. A way was now at hand to produce books in an inexpensive manner.

Unfortunately, things did not work out as Gutenberg had hoped. The church officials could not reach agreement on the text of the liturgy, so Gutenberg's original project did not come to fruition. He decided to print copies of the Bible instead, but he could not finance the amount of metal required, as well as the salaries of the skilled craftsmen needed to cut the master punches and produce the type, let alone the wages of the typesetters and the cost of the paper on which to print. He borrowed from a goldsmith-turned-venture-capitalist named Johann Fust, and started printing Bibles. Supposedly, just when the Bibles started rolling off the presses after some years of effort, Fust called in his loan. Fust got the Bibles and the press on which the Bibles were being printed, and thus got the present and future profits from the venture.

The most notable of the Bibles printed by Gutenberg is called by several names, including the Forty-two-line Bible, the Mazarin Bible, or sometimes simply the Gutenberg Bible. There were 30 original copies printed on vellum rather than ordinary paper, and only four are known to survive in their original form. The Bible had 1282 pages, and the best surviving vellum copy is called the Göttingen Bible. It has documentation that ties it to Gutenberg's first printing efforts. There were about 180 copies printed in total, and even the copies printed on paper have many hand-drawn embellishments. Each column of printing, with few exceptions, had 42 lines, hence the name "Forty-two-line Bible." The name Mazarin Bible comes from the fact that one well-preserved copy that gained great attention was found in the library of Cardinal Mazarin of France about two hundred years later in the 1600s.

The printing expertise demonstrated by Gutenberg spread quickly through Europe. Many of the skilled craftsmen involved with the first printing efforts got financing to open their own shops, as the technology was easily learned. By 1500 there were over 1,000 presses in existence. No matter who actually made the key invention in the mass production of printing books, some historians feel that this invention was in a sense irrelevant to the explosion of cheap books that followed. These historians feel that the invention was inevitable. They believe the real key to the beginning of the mass production of books came when Europeans learned how to make paper in large amounts, both precisely and cheaply.

Paper was originally invented in China, probably sometime around 100 A.D. The Chinese made their paper primarily with linen fibers taken from flax, and mixed with an excellent grade of vegetable gum. Chinese paper is very soft, but exceedingly tough. It is pure white, and it has a very even texture. The Arabs learned to make paper from the Chinese by supposedly extracting the secrets from Chinese men living in Turkestan. The Arabs became very good at papermaking and Arab manuscripts written on paper around the ninth century still exist. The Europeans found that paper was superior to the parchment which they had used to replace papyrus.

It has been conjectured that the capture of Moorish paper mills in Spain was the first step in bringing papermaking into Christian Europe. However it was done, by the end of the thirteenth century Italy was making excellent paper. The papermakers in Europe began to use clean linen rags instead of flax fibers to get the linen needed for the paper. This incidentally meant that from then on, rag pickers in Europe had a steady job. Also, animal glues were used for sizing instead of the vegetable gums used in China. Papermaking soon spread into Germany, and just before Gutenberg and other printers appeared on the scene, paper became readily available and cheap. This is why printing advances seemed inevitable. Books became cheap, which led to much more reading, which in turn enhanced the development of so-called "standard" Italian, English, French, Spanish, and German. As this process continued, it became possible to replace ancient Greek and Latin with the "standard" language of the particular country when discussing philosophy or science.

There is a popular "timeline" in science that is used to aid in the memorizing of the birth dates of certain famous people, and that also shows how one great mind replaced another in the evolutionary history of the world. Michelangelo, the great artist, sculptor, and scientist, was born in 1475 and died in 1564. In 1564 the great astronomer and scientist Galileo was born, and he died in 1642, the same year Sir Isaac Newton was born. The torch was properly passed in each case. Newton was quoted as saying:

> I don't know what I may seem to the world, but, as to myself, I seem to
> have been only like a boy, playing at the sea-shore, and diverting myself
> now and then finding a smoother pebble or a prettier shell than ordinary,
> whilst the great ocean of truth lay all undiscovered before me.

Newton felt the "ocean of truth" was partially to be discovered in books. Newton to a large extent was self-taught from his reading of books from all over the world. He was a prodigious reader, and at his death in 1727 he had over 2,000 books in his personal library (and a number of his own previously secret manuscripts). He said that if he seemed to see further than most people, it was because he stood on the shoulders of giants. Again it must be emphasized that the mass production of books that started in the late 1400s had the special value of teaching people what previous generations had learned, and not only the obvious value of increasing the degree of reading and enhancing the process of learning the basics of an education about present-day events.

An event took place in 1799 that enabled every nation to look back on prior generations in the history of Egypt. This was the discovery of the Rosetta stone. The French under Napoleon had invaded Egypt. While they were digging to add to a fort they had established near el-Rashid (founded as Rosetta in the ninth century), they discovered a granitoid (basalt) slab that had been inscribed by Egyptian priests around 200 B.C. (The stone was taken by the British in 1801 during war between Britain and France, and it now resides in the British Museum.)

The significance of the Rosetta stone, a decree from the reign of Ptolemy V, is that its text is written in three languages: hieroglyphics, demotic, and Greek. Hieroglyphics were slowly becoming obsolete at the time the stone was carved, and only priests still knew how to use them in their priestly decrees. Demotic (a kind of Arabic) was the basic script used in daily events, and Greek was the language of the administration (the period in Egyptian history after the death of Alexander the Great in 323 B.C. is known as the Macedonian dynasty).

This stone was crucial to our understanding of hieroglyphics because soon after the end of the fourth century, when hieroglyphics had gone out of use, the knowledge of how to read and write them was lost. With the discovery of the Rosetta stone it became possible to decipher the ancient hieroglyphics and to learn about the culture and history of Egypt. Thomas Young of Britain and Jean-François Champollion of France were the key figures in interpreting the Rosetta stone. Champollion was a scholar who could speak Greek, Latin, Hebrew, Arabic, Chaldean, and Syrian by the time he was 14, and he eventually founded the Egyptology Museum at the Louvre in Paris.

In the "time line" noted above, it could be added that another famous person was born in 1564, the same year as Galileo: William Shakespeare, whose famous plays in the Globe Theater in London became one of the first sources of mass entertainment/communication in the West. Shakespeare died in his early 50s in 1616. Now that mass printing was a routine process, the First Folio of his plays was printed in 1623. It is quite possible that some of the early settlers in the 1600s on their way to what would become the United States brought editions of his plays with them.

Before we begin to review the process of communication in the United States starting in the 1600s, we should review other forms of communication beyond writing and books that had been established before settlers arrived here. Greek soldiers once sent messages by turning a shield toward the sun, creating a pattern of flashes that other Greek soldiers could decode but the enemy could not. Roman soldiers took a more "brute force" approach by building long rows of signal towers. Their soldiers would simply shout the messages from tower to tower, thus spreading field instructions rapidly over a distance. Native Americans long sent messages by smoke signals, building a smoky fire on a hill and using a blanket to release puffs of smoke at the proper intervals. They also used a system similar to the one originally thought to have been developed in Africa, where a series of drums were kept in hearing distance of the next set. Coded drum signals could send messages at great speed for hundreds of miles. In Europe, men climbed towers to send messages using a semaphore system. Adapting this system to ships, where a series of flags were used to spell the message, was a logical next step.

As many methods as can be imagined were used to send messages because the development of writing did not solve the problem of communicating quickly over a long distance. Nearly all of the developments in communications after 1800 in the United States would address this issue. The solutions would lead step by step to today's Internet and its related methods of communication.

Permanent settlers began to arrive in the United States in the early 1600s, setting up an establishment at Jamestown in Virginia in 1607, and a more famous one in Plymouth, Massachusetts, in 1620. These settlers were accustomed to books and writing, and immediately began communicating by letters and messages delivered by couriers of various kinds. In 1672 a monthly postal system was established between the cities of New York and Boston. Twenty years later, the British postmaster general confirmed a postmaster general for the American colonies, and official national mail service was launched.

The first American newspaper was published at almost the same time, in 1690 in Boston. It was called *Publick Occurrences Both Foreign and Domestick*, but it was published only once because the authorities were outraged that it was published without a proper license. Fourteen years later, in 1704, the postmaster general of Boston, John Campbell (who was also a bookseller), published the *Boston News-Letter*. Several other papers followed as new postmasters general were appointed. One of these newspapers was assembled by a young Benjamin Franklin, filling in for his brother James Franklin. Once he became legally free of being an apprentice, Franklin broke with his brother, whom he disliked, and ended up eventually in Philadelphia.

Benjamin Franklin and a partner started publishing the *Pennsylvania Gazette* in 1729. By the following year, Franklin was the sole owner, and in 1732 he began publishing his famous *Poor Richard's Almanac*, which was a great success for the next 25 years. Franklin was also a bookseller and inventor, and he established a circulating library. By 1748 his publishing activities were so successful that he turned his printing business over to his foreman, expecting to dedicate the rest of his life to science. But instead Franklin was soon called to devote his considerable talents to the service of his country, which in just a few decades was to become the United States.

Franklin also wrote letters of introduction for an Englishman named Tom Paine, who came to the colonies in 1774. Paine became very interested in the talk of revolution brewing in the colonies, and in January 1776 he wrote a pamphlet called *Common Sense* in which he appealed to the "common man" to declare independence. Soon more than 100,000 copies were in circulation, and the pamphlet had a great impact on the public in general and on the members of the Continental Congress in Philadelphia, where the pamphlet was originally published. Over the seven years following the Declaration of Independence, Paine wrote a series of 16 pamphlets called The American Crisis which encouraged the revolutionaries in their battle against England. It is not too much to say that Paine was the key person using his communication talents to help start and sustain the Revolution.

Thomas Jefferson is given the major credit for writing the Declaration of Independence, but his draft was much altered in a Congressional session on July 3, 1776, the day after Congress had voted to declare independence from England. The key phrases that most remember, however, were published as originally submitted by Jefferson, although Benjamin Franklin and John Adams provided advice to Jefferson as he wrote the original draft. Thus, Thomas Paine and Thomas Jefferson can be credited with creating the words used in the mass communications that led to the revolutionary birth of the United States.

In 1790, as the United States tried to take its place among the nations of the world, Alexander Hamilton, then secretary of the treasury, proposed that the United States redeem all "Continentals," the paper money issued by Congress during the revolution, and, in addition, that the federal government should assume the debts of the individual states. These two steps would create financial credibility in the eyes of the world for both the individual states and the federal government. It was agreed to do so, but 80 million dollars in bonds (an immense sum in 1790) would have to be issued to underwrite the process. The selling of these bonds to the public would eventually lead to the creation of the New York Stock Exchange (NYSE).

Once the NYSE was established, the demand for more rapid communication between the NYSE and other exchanges in the world, as well as for more rapid knowledge of news in general that might affect the price of securities, began to become more insistent. Another result of the lack of rapid communications was the last battle fought in the War of 1812, the battle of New Orleans (1815). It was a great victory for the United States, in which marksmen from the countryside under Andrew Jackson inflicted high casualties on the British troops marching in their usual close-order fashion. More than 1,000 soldiers were killed or wounded, the majority of them British. However, the battle should have never been fought: peace had been declared between the countries two weeks before the first shot was fired in New Orleans.

The NYSE was so desperate for speedier communications in the early 1800s that a private semaphore service was set up between the New York and Philadelphia stock exchanges. Agents were stationed every six or eight miles on the tops of tall buildings. Telescopes were used to read the flag signals, and each agent sent the news onward. It took only about 30 minutes to send information over the 90 miles between New York and Philadelphia, although bad weather was obviously a problem. When the telegraph was developed for commercial use about 1844, the semaphore service was disbanded.

The Telegraph

Samuel Morse is credited as the inventor of the telegraph as well as the "Morse code" that was used to transmit messages over the telegraph. But as is usually the case with such inventions, other inventors, especially in Europe, had anticipated much of Morse's work, and even his code was similar to other codes, including those used in some semaphore systems. However, Morse persisted for 12 years in developing his system, starting in 1832, and he tried to interest investors in the United States, Europe, and Russia between 1838 and 1844 to back his prototype. No one would do so until he obtained some money from the U.S. Congress and sent his famous first telegraph message in 1844. So if there were other inventors who were "close" to his idea, they had plenty of time to produce something. Morse deserves credit for his persistence, if nothing else.

Morse started out as a painter, became well known as a portrait painter, and was one of the founders of the National Academy of Design in 1825. He had gone to England twice to study art, and it was on his return from England in 1832 that he was told by another passenger on the ship of electricity and electromagnetism experiments taking place in Europe. Morse supposedly had a dream that night that led him to the design of the telegraph, and before he left the ship Morse had worked out his basic "Morse code." However, Morse had been interested in electricity since his college days, and had attended many lectures on the subject. Also, by 1832 he was aware of Ampère's idea for an electric telegraph (Ampère is the man after whom the unit of electric current is named).

Morse started working on his telegraph design as soon as he was back in the United States, and he got help from some other men, but capital was hard to raise for field tests. He taught art at college to support himself, and one of his students became interested in the telegraph. The student had a rich father, and the father gave Morse enough money to build a small laboratory. The father was skeptical of the whole affair, however, and once gave his son a message reading, "a patient waiter is no loser," and had his son tap out the message to send to Morse who was in the next room. When Morse wrote out the message correctly, the father was impressed — but not to the extent of funding the new invention. It was clear Morse's model worked as claimed, but what was needed was a test in an operating system, and that would take the construction of a telegraph line. Funds would be needed to build such a system. Even a successful demonstration for President Martin Van Buren on February 21, 1838, failed to raise the funds, even though the government had previously established a prize of $30,000 for an operating system of some sort along the East Coast.

Morse persevered in trying to get his first telegraph line built. Morse finally convinced Congress to give him the $30,000 in 1843 to build an experimental line between Washington and Baltimore. Morse had a setback when the wire bought for the project turned out to be improperly insulated, and it essentially shorted out in the pipes used to install it underground. Morse had already spent $20,000 of the original grant, but with the remaining $10,000 he was able to string the line on poles and trees, insulating the wires by using the necks of glass bottles. The final line was about 40 miles long.

On the appointed day, May 24, 1844, the daughter of the commissioner of patents selected the message "What hath God wrought?" It was tapped out in Washington, received in Baltimore and retransmitted to Washington to confirm it had been received properly. Conducted before a crowd of newspaper reporters, the experiment was deemed a success. Almost immediately telegraph lines sprang up between cities in the United States and Europe. The age of instant communication at a distance had arrived. Except perhaps for the arrival of cheap printed books in the later 1400s, it was the first major change in communications since the time of the Roman Empire nearly 2000 years earlier.

The telegraph required the construction of telegraph lines, and it took time for this to happen across the vastness of the United States, although it took place very rapidly along the densely populated eastern seaboard. When gold was discovered in 1848 in California, there became an urgent need for fast communications between East and West. In the years just before a coast-to-coast telegraph line was constructed, America saw one of the more romantic episodes in its history: the Pony Express. After constant complaints about the delay in getting news to and from California, a private enterprise was established in 1860 to get mail quickly between the city of St. Joseph in Missouri (essentially the westernmost terminus of telegraph lines and train travel in the United States) and Sacramento in California. The head of the enterprise, William H. Russell, placed a classic advertisement in selected newspapers in March 1860. It read: "Wanted: Young, skinny, wiry fellows, not over 18. Must be expert riders willing to risk death daily. Orphans preferred." The Pony Express carried the mail over its 2,000-mile route in about 10 days, half the time taken by the overland stage that took the southern route to California. The Pony Express operated from April 1860 to October 1861, then went out of business when the transcontinental telegraph line was completed in 1861.

The telegraph was also critical in the building of the transcontinental railroad between 1863 and 1869. Congress required the railroads to build a telegraph line along the railroad right-of-way as the new railroad was constructed. The prime method of communication between the builders of the railroads and their suppliers at each end was the telegraph. It is not too much to say that if there were no telegraph, railroad construction would have taken years longer.

Meanwhile, the telegraph had been such a success nationally that thoughts soon turned to laying a telegraph line under the ocean to get instant communication between the United States and Great Britain, and thence to the continent of Europe. Again the stock market was a prime mover for the line. Fortunes could be made there based on having key news just a few minutes earlier than anybody else. For a while in the 1850s, a businessman based in Boston would travel to Nova Scotia to board steamers headed for the United States. He would read European newspapers on the ship and talk to the passengers, and then send a summary of what he considered significant news to Boston via carrier pigeons he had brought on board with him. The subscribers to his service thus got the news some days before it would normally be available. The telegraph made it possible to transmit his news instantly from Boston to New York.

Aware of this need, a young businessman named Cyrus Field put together a group of investors to lay a cable under the Atlantic Ocean. Both the American and British governments agreed to work with Field's company. In 1857 an American ship, the *Niagara*, sailed east, and a British ship, the *Agamemnon*, sailed west. The two ships each were to lay out half the cable needed, meet in mid-ocean, and splice the two cables. But each ship had its cable break, and the same thing happened again in 1858. Finally, on the fifth attempt, a line was successfully laid between Newfoundland and Ireland and the first message was sent on August 16, 1858. General euphoria followed, and President Buchanan and Queen Victoria exchanged dots and dashes of congratulations. But the cable stopped working only three weeks after it had been laid.

It turned out that Scottish scientist James Thomson (later Lord Kelvin), who had been hired by Field as a consultant on the project, had designed and patented a highly sensitive receiver to be used for the low-level signals that he had calculated would come out at the end of the cable after traveling more than 2,000 miles and suffering inevitable losses in strength along the way. However, Thomson's approach had been overruled by others. Field organized another effort after the Civil War ended in 1865, and this time Field appointed Thomson the chief engineer on the project.

In 1865, the largest ship in the world, the *Great Eastern*, was used to attempt another cable laying, but the cable broke after about 1,200 miles had been spooled out. Field raised more money, the biggest and strongest cable in history was built, and in July 1866 the *Great Eastern* sailed again. This cable did not break, and once communications had been established between Ireland and Newfoundland, the cable went on working indefinitely: no big fade out this time after a big celebration.

Queen Victoria knighted Thomson for his efforts, and Thomson later took the name Lord Kelvin when he became a baron in 1892. The Kelvin temperature scale starting at -273 degrees centigrade is named after him for his work in the study of heat and heat energy, part of which was his discovery of absolute zero and the second law of thermodynamics. A burst of cable-laying followed the successful laying of the cable between Ireland and Newfoundland in 1866, and as Thomson/Kelvin held the patents on the design of the cable and his sensitive receiver, he became a wealthy man. Nevertheless he maintained his post as professor of physics at the University of Glasgow until he was 75, following a tenure of 53 years in the position (he was 42 when the cable was successfully laid in 1866). Thomson is one of the few true scientists who became both famous and wealthy from his work, and who lived long enough (he died in 1907) to see how the world had changed as a result of his efforts.

The world changed in many ways because of the telegraph. Telegraph lines were covering the land and lying on the bottom of the ocean, bringing essentially instantaneous communication around the globe. But also, as we have seen, the development of the telegraph was not so much a question of designing a working model as of convincing people to invest in the construction of the telegraph lines. Morse's telegraph was not much different from that of many other designers, but he persisted in getting the test line built. Now that the construction hurdle had been cleared, many other inventors began working to improve Morse's basically simple design. It was this effort that led to the next great advance in communications, the telephone.

The Telephone

Alexander Graham Bell, who is credited with inventing the telephone in 1876, was born in Scotland and came to the United States (Boston) via Canada in 1871. He had been both a music and speech teacher and had worked with the deaf and people with hearing disabilities. He started out to improve the telegraph so that it could transmit several sounds at once because he thought he could use it to help people with hearing disabilities learn to speak. Studying and testing an eardrum he had obtained from a Boston ear specialist, Bell recognized that a thin steel diaphragm could do the same thing in the "telegraph" he was trying to build to conduct a range of sounds over its wire. He also recognized immediately that such a system could conduct the full range of sounds produced by the human voice. Since he was limited in his mechanical abilities, he hired an electrical mechanic named Thomas A. Watson, and set out to reduce his ideas to practice.

On February 14, 1876, Bell applied for a patent based on his ideas to that date. The most difficult part to reduce to practice was the transmitter. The patent, which turned out to be the most lucrative single patent in history, was granted on March 7, 1876. Bell and Watson had been working furiously since filing their patent application to prove that the idea actually worked. On March 10, 1876, they were getting ready to try a crucial test. Bell, working on the transmitter end of the phone, accidentally spilled some acid on his clothes and quickly called for Watson, who was three rooms away waiting on a receiver, to come help. Watson heard the call clearly. It was the first telephone call.

It happened that another inventor, Elisha Gray, had filed a "caveat" (an intention to file a patent later) only two hours after Bell's patent had been filed on February 14, 1876. But Gray was also having trouble determining how to make the transmitter part of the telephone work, and he did not pursue his effort as feverishly as Bell. In fact, after learning of Bell's success, he simply gave up the effort. Gray later challenged Bell in court claiming his caveat more closely described the final telephone that was actually developed than Bell's patent did, but Bell won in court. Gray had founded an electric manufacturing company in 1869 that was later known as the Western Electric Manufacturing Company. Ironically, in 1881, the new Bell Telephone Company acquired a controlling interest in Western Electric to build its new telephones. The Western Electric Company became one of the world's largest and most profitable companies. But Gray left the company in 1881 to return to his alma mater, Oberlin College, to teach and conduct research. A difference of only two hours means it is the Bell Telephone Company we talk about today instead of the Gray Telephone Company.

After his March 10, 1876, success, Bell next demonstrated his working invention at the American Academy of Arts and Sciences in Boston on May 10, 1876. But as with the telegraph, much money would be required to build the infrastructure of telephone poles and wires and so forth, and no substantial investors were forthcoming. Bell was then pressured by friends and a few backers to exhibit his new invention at the great Centennial Exposition taking place in Philadelphia to honor the 100th anniversary of the birth of the United States. There would be a prize for the most important and exciting invention displayed at the Exposition, but there were so many inventors displaying their creations at the Exposition (including the Otto four-stroke internal combustion engine that would form the basis of the new "horseless carriage" automotive industry soon to be born in the United States) that little notice was given to Bell and his invention.

Then on Sunday, June 25, 1876, a group of judges walking listlessly through the hot, humid Exhibition Hall, ready to leave due to the heat, were directed to Bell's corner of the hall by Dom Pedro II, the emperor of Brazil, who was one of the judges and who had met Bell before. The judges gathered around the receiving end while Bell walked some distance away and then spoke into a transmitter. Depending on the source, Dom Pedro then shouted either "I hear! I hear!" or "It talks! It talks!" Either way, the other judges got a chance to listen and Bell's telephone became the most popular invention at the Exposition. After that, money was easier to raise from investors who now could detect the smell of money coming from the telephone.

By July 9, 1877, the Bell Telephone Company had been formed. The first telephone exchange was established in New Haven, Connecticut, in 1878, and as improvements were made that made it easier to use the telephone, both telephones and exchanges grew rapidly. When the brand-new stock exchange was built in 1903, there were 500 telephones installed around the trading floor. One of the major advantages that the telephone had over the telegraph is that the telephone quickly evolved into what we call now a "user-friendly" system. People could pick up the telephone in their home and call someone else in *their* home. No one thought about putting a telegraph in their home. One had to know how to operate a telegraph using the proper code, and the person on the other end had to know the same things. To send a telegraph one had to go to a telegraph station, and the response could only be received at the telegraph station, or via a messenger from the station. Every home in America became a potential market for a telephone, as did every business. Use of the telephone grew exponentially. A century later, the introduction of the personal computer would change the world in much the same way.

The invention of the telephone was the fundamental basis for many of the inventions that followed in the next 125 years. The vibrations of the human voice were converted into electrical signals at the speaker's end, and converted back at the listener's end. This basic principle still holds. The manner in which the electrical signals are transmitted has changed greatly, from wires to satellites to fiber-optics, but the basic principle of the telephone transmission is essentially unchanged. We have developed better ways to make telephones and their associated equipment using transistors and semiconductor chips and so forth, and we also have developed the computer and created ways for computers to talk to each other. However, we are still converting speech (or data or pictures) to electrical impulses that are transmitted in various ways, and then converted back to speech (or data or pictures) when the transmissions arrive at the intended point. In this sense we have to consider the telephone, which was originally developed by persons trying to improve or expand the use of the telegraph, as one of the most fundamental inventions in the history of the world, as well as the history of communications.

The telephone and telephone system both underwent many improvements in the decades after the Bell Telephone Company was formed in 1876. The company grew as the United States grew, and after weathering hard times in the depression of the 1930s just as the country did, Bell Telephone became a colossus. By 1939, the Bell Telephone Company had a net worth of five billion dollars, the largest amount of money ever controlled by a single private company to that time.

The Movies and the Phonograph

While the world's attention in general was being captured by the invention of the telegraph and the telephone, several other events took place in the 1800s that were important in the history of communication, especially mass communication. We noted the early beginning of the publication of newspapers in the United States, but up until the 1800s, newspapers were generally written for the "upper class" and intended to be sold through relatively limited subscription lists (sometimes as few as several hundred copies). The growth of education for everyone and the increased concentration of the population in the cities led to a new approach. The "penny press" approach, demonstrated by such newspapers as the *New York Sun* in the 1830s, featured newspapers written for mass consumption and sold in the streets for one penny each. Sales climbed into the thousands and then into the millions. The concept of writing for the masses not only broadened the range of news carried in the newspapers, but led to advances in printing technology to increase the speed of printing while lowering the costs. Marketing gimmicks aimed at increasing the circulation of the paper became commonplace. By the 1890s some mass-oriented newspapers boasted of a circulation of over one million copies, and the idea of mass media consumption had been well established in the United States.

Thomas A. Edison, who soon would develop the electric light bulb and a host of related products, came out with what we now call the phonograph in 1877. Edison called his device a "talking machine" which, following the lead of Bell's telephone, impressed the vibrations of human speech on a rotating cylinder. The marks caused by the vibrations would play back the original speech when fed through the proper "decoding" device. Edison meant his invention to be used as a dictating machine in business, and he was insulted when others saw its great potential as a machine to be used for mass entertainment. He did not want to be involved with inventing a "toy."

By 1886 an improved version of the cylinder, which included the use an electric motor to drive it at a steady speed that Edison had developed in 1878, was introduced by Edison and some new partners (one of whom was a cousin of Alexander Graham Bell). The cylinders were bought by a ready public who wanted to hear the recordings of great artists. In 1887, German-born Emil Berliner, an American citizen, invented flat disks rather than cylinders to be used for the same purpose in what he called the gramophone. His system became the standard by the turn of the century. Berliner returned to Germany in 1888 and founded a company there that even today is one of the world's most important classical music recording companies.

The gramophone system, using the flat disks that would eventually be known as records, flourished in the United States. By 1920, over two hundred manufacturers were building more than two million machines a year, and the records to go with them. The machines were enclosed in lovely wood cabinets, and were given a place of prominence in the home. This would make it easy for RCA to put radios in those cabinets within the next decade.

Before radio appeared on the scene, master inventor Thomas Edison devised, in 1889, what he called the Kinetoscope. This was the first practical movie projector, but so many people had been working so long on this effort that there is some suspicion that Edison simply put his highly marketable name on what others had done. The basic principle underlying motion pictures, the persistence of vision, had been known since the time of Leonardo da Vinci around 1500. When still pictures of a certain sequence of events are viewed at the proper speed, the eye, retaining for an instant the last image it has seen, will perceive the illusion of motion. Since the early 1800s people had viewed various images printed on an opaque surface through a spinning wheel or disk that gave the illusion of viewing pictures that moved. Edison's big breakthrough was to print images on a transparent material that could be *projected*.

Edison combined breakthroughs in film being created by George Eastman (founder of Eastman Kodak) around the same time, and Edison patented the two elements of the basic motion picture system in 1891. One patent was for his Kinetograph, the first camera meant to specifically film motion pictures, and the second was for his Kinetoscope, the first movie projector as noted above. By 1893 the system debuted in New York as a sort of "peep show" which only one person could view at a time. Edison did not patent these inventions in Europe, so two French brothers built on them to produce the Cinematographie, which projected films on a theater wall in Paris on March 22, 1895. Edison responded by improving his invention so that films could also be projected in a large-scale process. He called his new invention the Vitascope, and films were shown in a theater for the first time in the United States at Bial's Music Hall in New York on April 23, 1896. Later that year a former associate of Edison developed the Biograph to further improve large-scale projection, and a company called American Biograph was the first real motion picture production company even though Edison had built a movie studio in 1893.

"Movies" were an instant success, rising from the "Nickelodeons" around the turn of the century to the silent-film days featuring Charlie Chaplin and other such stars into the 1920s. Movies were the ultimate mass-communication medium at the time. But the movie industry was so satisfied with its success that it did little to pursue the development of "talkies" until radio had risen to popularity in the 1920s. Then the radio king, RCA, became involved with providing sound to movies in 1928. The marriage between what we now call "broadcasting" and the film industry began in earnest in that year. But to discuss the rise of radio and broadcasting, we have to go back to the 1870s once more. The development of what was called wireless radio transmission started in this period, and the development of radio itself as well as television followed relatively quickly.

Wireless Communication, the Radio, and Television

Even before Bell had filed his patent for the telephone in 1876, a famous Scottish physicist named James Clerk Maxwell published a paper in 1873 predicting the existence of invisible radiant energy similar to light. Maxwell claimed that, based on everything known about light, his calculations showed that electromagnetic radiation in the form of waves must exist throughout the frequency spectrum. More than twelve years later, a German scientist named Heinrich Hertz conducted experiments in which he generated and detected such waves. The waves came to be known as Hertzian or radio waves, and the measure of the frequency of such waves was named the Hertz; one Hertz is one cycle per second.

Many scientists began experimenting with such waves, and many countries claim to have invented radio based on the experimental work of their scientists. However, radio as we understand it now was not fully developed until about 1920. What scientists were developing in the 1890s, after Hertz published a paper about his experiments in 1888, was wireless communication. In this form of communication, information is transmitted via "radio waves" without any intervening wires. The immediate application of this form of transmission was sending and receiving the dots and dashes of the telegraphic code to and from ships at sea, both to each other and from ship to shore. The use of radio waves to send radio signals (and later television and radar signals, etc.) was still in the future as of the 1890s.

Probably the most famous experimenter of this time was an Italian inventor named Guglielmo Marconi. At the age of 21 in 1895, Marconi transmitted a message via radio waves over a distance of one and one-half miles on the grounds of his father's estate in Italy. Both of Marconi's parents were independently wealthy, and Marconi had both the time and the funds to immerse himself in experimentation. Marconi's many successful experiments convinced him that wireless transmission was going to be much more than just a toy, and he tried to interest the Italian government, without success, in his work. As Marconi's mother was a member of a family of well-known Irish whiskey distillers, she arranged for Marconi to go to London under the auspices of English postal (England's postal systems were in charge of all communications in the country) and military officials. Marconi filed a patent there in 1896, when he was only 22.

Frustrated by the long delay caused by bureaucratic problems in having the interested British officials apply for a license for his patent, Marconi started his own company in London in 1897 with the help of his mother's connections. The first customer for the communication products of the Marconi Company was the British government for use in the Boer War in South Africa. Marconi transmitted signals across the English Channel in 1899, and in 1901 he sent the first transatlantic signals across the 2000 miles between England and Newfoundland. He shared the Nobel Prize in physics in 1909 for his work in "wireless telegraphy."

Marconi was an attractive man, raised very much in the continental manner of the rich, and he was a big hit in the United States when he opened the American Marconi branch of his business in 1899. By 1913 the company was making good profits. In that year Marconi acquired the assets of the bankrupt United Wireless Company, once under the direction of the American inventor Lee De Forest, who invented the Audion tube in 1906 and patented it in 1907. This acquisition gave Marconi a virtual monopoly on wireless communication in the United States. Marconi had 17 land stations and 400 ship-based stations but all of these stations were used for point-to-point telegraphic communications between ships or from ship to shore.

The invention of the so-called audion, which was the first vacuum tube to use a grid, was a key element of what finally led to the radio itself. However, the audion was first used in telephone systems. In 1913 Bell Telephone bought rights, limited to telephonic applications, to De Forest's invention in 1913 for use in amplifying long-distance telephone signals. This was typical of a number of inventions made originally to improve wireless communication. In 1913, Edwin H. Armstrong patented the circuit for the regenerative receiver that made long-range radio-wave reception practicable. The crystal detector was introduced in 1903 and was in general use by 1906. This would become the famous "cat whisker" of early radio. Marconi obtained yet another patent in 1904 for a "tuner" to greatly improve reception in wireless communication.

The technological elements of radio as we know it now were all in place before the United States entered World War I in 1917. Radio was essentially an "invention" of a concept rather than the invention of a specific product. The person who was a prime mover in creating the concept of radio was David Sarnoff, a Russian immigrant who joined American Marconi as a teenager. As a 21-year-old telegraph operator he happened to be on duty when the "unsinkable" *Titanic* sank on its maiden voyage on April 14, 1912. The romantic story that emerged later of how Sarnoff stayed at his post single-handedly for 72 hours to bring news of the sinking of the *Titanic* and a listing of its survivors has been questioned in many of its details, but the story and its detractors all came after the fact. What is unquestioned is that wireless communication became incredibly popular after the *Titanic* event, and Sarnoff began a rapid rise into the executive levels of American Marconi.

During the First World War, the United States had been able to pursue its wireless communication efforts only by forcing the many conflicting patent holders to join in a cross-licensing pool (as it had done in the new aircraft industry). After the war ended in 1918, the armed forces were unhappy at the prospect of returning control to a "foreign" power in the form of American Marconi. President Wilson and his advisors realized that the balance of power in the world now depended on who controlled communications, oil, and shipping. Great Britain controlled the oceans while the United States had the highest oil production. Since Great Britain had long controlled cable communications, with the Marconi Company they would have a near-monopoly in wireless communications. Pressure was brought to have American Marconi sell out to General Electric, already a big communications equipment manufacturer, with the understanding that GE would continue to sell certain critical items to Marconi for use outside the United States. GE then created a subsidiary called the Radio Corporation of America (RCA) to carry on the activities of American Marconi. RCA was created November 20, 1919, and GE, Westinghouse, and American Telephone and Telegraph (AT&T — the transmission unit of Bell Telephone) were the basic holders of RCA stock. But none of these companies were yet thinking of radios and radio broadcasting. Their focus was continued wireless communication for point-to-point applications such as ship to ship and ship to shore.

David Sarnoff joined RCA when the American Marconi operation was absorbed. Sarnoff had written what has been called his "music box" memo to his American Marconi supervisors in 1916. Sarnoff foresaw that wireless communication could turn into a "broadcasting" phenomenon. Previously, wireless communication was always thought of as a "point-to-point" medium, as had telegraphy and the telephone before it. Someone always sent a message to someone, and revenue was easy to derive at the point of transmission or reception. But Sarnoff saw that information could also be broadcast over the air to many unknown receivers. The "messages" could include entertainment such as music, and revenues would be derived from selling the "music boxes" to those who wanted to receive the transmissions. An additional source of revenue could be the sale of advertising on the transmitted programs.

Others had thought about this approach before, but it was truly a new concept in the general field of communications. Signals were sent essentially at random to those willing to buy a receiver to receive whatever was transmitted. This concept was the founding of radio as we know it now, and later of television. Some think Sarnoff's key memo was written in 1920 when Sarnoff wrote a 28-page memo to the chairman of RCA, who was also a key man at GE, proposing this same approach. Sarnoff predicted that RCA could sell a million receiving sets in three years if it acted quickly. The patents needed to enable the "radio" and radio broadcasting to begin were held by the three companies founding RCA — GE (which held the prior American Marconi patents as well as many of its own), Westinghouse, and AT&T. The patents would have to be pooled and cross-licensed as they had been by the government during the war.

Westinghouse got started first when one of its engineers, Frank Conrad, began in 1920 to transmit music regularly to the many amateur operators who routinely listened in on wireless transmissions intended for ships at sea. The Horne Department Store in Pittsburgh took notice of the popularity of Conrad's transmissions, set up a demonstration receiver in its store, and ran an advertisement on September 22, 1920, saying that amateur receiving sets like the one in its store could be bought "for $10 and up." Then Westinghouse converted a radiotelegraph transmitter to be used for what was then known as radiotelephony and went on the air as radio station KDKA on November 2, 1920. Their first official broadcast provided news about the Warren Harding–James Cox presidential election, interspersed with phonograph music and selections from a live banjo player. The first regular radio program had been born.

Other experimental stations later claimed the honor of being first (an experimental test had been made as early as 1906, and it startled operators on ships at sea as they heard voices and music emerging from the ether instead of dots and dashes), but KDKA was the first to broadcast on a regular basis and to be licensed by the government as a transmitting station. The KDKA experiment was so successful everybody wanted to get in on the act. By the end of 1920, 30 stations had been licensed. By 1922 the number of licensed stations was approaching 600. The number of radio sets sold soared into the hundreds of thousands by the end of 1922.

One of the reasons for the strong demand for radio sets was David Sarnoff's realization that popular events would have to be broadcast on radio to stimulate people to want to own sets. In the summer of 1921, Sarnoff orchestrated a great publicity stunt by planning to broadcast the Jack Dempsey–Georges Carpentier fight for the heavyweight championship of the world. Dempsey was cast as the scowling villain who had been accused of draft dodging. On the other side was the handsome Carpentier, the French champion who had been a decorated combat pilot. Sarnoff got a powerful new transmitter made by GE delivered to the site of the fight, a place called Boyle's Thirty Acres in northern New Jersey, just over the Hudson River from New

York. (The transmitter had been made for the Navy but was diverted temporarily to the fight with the help of the ex-assistant secretary of the Navy, Franklin D. Roosevelt.) Then Sarnoff turned the fight into a charity event, with proceeds from people who paid their way into "listening events" in halls and theaters everywhere going to favorite charities of Anne Morgan, daughter of financier Pierpont Morgan, and Franklin D. Roosevelt. Both of these famous figures helped to promote the listening parties set up for the event.

Sarnoff acquired 300 big "tulip" horns meant to be attached to phonographs, and had them attached to radios by his engineers so that crowds of people could hear each radio, which at that time were designed to be listened to by one person using earphones. Over 90,000 people came to see the fight on July 2, 1921, the biggest crowd ever to see a sporting event up to that date. An estimated 300,000 people heard the radio broadcast including listeners up to 500 miles away. As in nearly all stories about Sarnoff, the degree of his involvement might not have been what he later claimed, but he was clearly involved in some way and the broadcast of the fight was a great success — as was the fight itself, which Dempsey won with a knockout in the fourth round.

Sales of radio sets grew faster than anyone could have imagined. Herbert Hoover, then secretary of commerce, announced in 1922 what he called "one of the most astonishing things" he had seen in American life: during 1922 the Department of Commerce estimated that somewhere between 600,000 and one million persons now owned radio sets compared to less than 50,000 only a year before. RCA rode the surge upward and became the top dog in the business by both selling radios and collecting licensing fees on the patents it controlled (more than 200 radio manufacturers and 5,000 parts distributors had sprung up to take part in the rapidly growing industry). One of the advantages of radio compared to prior communications inventions was that it required no associated infrastructure like poles and wires. One simply bought the box, took it home, and turned it on to listen.

Among flurries of patent infringement suits and antitrust issues, RCA under Sarnoff's visionary direction also created the first radio broadcasting network, the National Broadcasting Company (NBC). NBC had so many stations available that it created a "red" and a "blue" network (the blue network was sold decades later to the American Broadcasting Company (ABC) due to antitrust issues). NBC started service on November 15, 1926, but did not become fully operational until 1927. By then, a second network eventually named the Columbia Broadcasting System (CBS) had struggled into existence. It was taken over by William S. Paley in 1928, and it ceased to struggle and became (and remained) a significant competitor to NBC. Bill Paley was the son of a wealthy cigar manufacturer, and he came to radio by way of being the advertising manager for his father's cigar business. He tried radio advertising, liked the results, and moved into radio as the head of his own network. He was responsible for many innovations in network operation, most later copied by NBC, and the names of Sarnoff and Paley became synonymous with broadcasting of both radio and television for the rest of both men's lives.

The next big step in communication after radio and broadcasting networks were established was the advent of television. An individual inventor named Philo T. Farnsworth finally won the patent battle for television, but RCA won the war. Farnsworth won a court decision announced in July 1935 giving him priority for his patents that he had originally filed on January 7, 1927, and after, but Farnsworth was not as good a businessman as David Sarnoff. At the World's Fair in April 1939, RCA kicked off the television age by exhibiting television sets created by RCA and demonstrating their use. Sarnoff knew he would have to come to some agreement with Farnsworth, who owned the basic patent rights even though Vladimir Zworkin of RCA had created his own essential components for the RCA television system. It should be noted that some references credit John Baird, a Scottish inventor living in England, for creating the first television system in 1923, but this was a mechanical system based on a spinning disk that never produced a resolution that was acceptable for wide use. Both Farnsworth and Zworkin were working with electronic scanning which led to television as we know it now.

Sarnoff's bold stroke at the 1939 World's Fair identified RCA with the birth of television, but it soon became academic as World War II meant the end of the production of consumer electronics for the duration. RCA did settle with Farnsworth early in September 1939, just as Nazi troops marched into Poland. The Federal Communications Commission (FCC) set standards for broadcasting commercial television in April 1941, just a little over seven months before the Japanese attack on Pearl Harbor.

After the war, television caught on even more strongly than radio had 25 years earlier. Starting in the fall of 1947, consumers bought one million sets in two years. The market was 80 percent controlled by RCA. On January 7, 1949, NBC showed a program celebrating the 25th anniversary of television, referring to a patent claimed by Vladimir Zworkin on December 29, 1923. Sarnoff was later dubbed officially the "Father of Television" and Zworkin the "Inventor of Television." Farnsworth's key patents expired in 1947, and his television manufacturing company was unable to compete with the 75 companies manufacturing television sets by 1948. Farnsworth was gone from the television scene by 1949. He was not the first, and surely not the last, inventor whose business skills failed to match his inventing skills.

Jumping a little ahead of our story, RCA was ultimately run into the ground by Bobby Sarnoff, the son of David Sarnoff. Bobby Sarnoff tried unsuccessfully to turn RCA into a conglomerate involved in many business areas. In what has to rank as an ironic transaction, GE acquired RCA in 1986.

GE was the first owner of RCA in 1919, then had to divest its remaining share in the early 1930s as part of an antitrust action. GE paid $6.3 billion for RCA as it was in 1986, then proceeded to sell off its pieces until only NBC was left, and GE decided to hold onto NBC. The dramatic change in communications in the United States brought about by radio and then television was muted by the end of the century, as the Japanese and other Asian manufacturers took over the radio and television product markets. The independent networks had disappeared, with NBC going to GE, CBS going to Westinghouse, and ABC going to Disney. Television advertising would become a $50 billion business by the end of the century, surpassing newspapers for the first time as the nation's top marketing medium. Further, Americans watched television about four hours a day, making television the nation's favorite "leisure time" activity. So the great inventions from the telegraph through television have continued to change our lives in many ways, even though the key players have changed.

The story of communications after the war has also changed greatly, and that story begins with the invention of the tiny transistor in 1948. In many ways the post-war changes in communications have not been driven by the invention of new things, but rather by the invention of new ways to do things we were already doing. Those "new ways" were so dramatically different that by 2000 they had changed our methods of communicating in ways we could not imagine in 1950, but those new ways were essentially "only" the conversion of the elements of communication from wires and solder and vacuum tubes to the world of semiconductors.

In January 1948, the Bell Telephone Research Laboratories announced that they had invented what they called the "transistor," although the precise date of the invention was the month before, December 16, 1947. The name was selected because the inventors said the device "transferred" a current across a semiconductor "resistor." The exact source of the name is irrelevant. What the inventors had done was similar in impact to the invention of the steam engine in 1769. The steam engine essentially gave rise to the industrial revolution and all that followed. The transistor gave birth to the world of semiconductors and all that followed in the general field of electronics, and specifically in the world of communications. Thus the three inventors of the transistor — John Bardeen, Walter Brittain, and William Shockley, who shared the Nobel Prize in 1956 for their work — actually kicked off the world of semiconductor product manufacturing, and in this way gave rise to satellite communications, integrated circuits, the microprocessor and personal computer, and the Internet. Quite a legacy for anyone.

A semiconductor is exactly what it sounds like, a "semi" conductor. Metal, like copper, is a good conductor of electricity. A brick is a non-conductor of electricity. A material like silicon, properly "doped" with certain impurities, is a semiconductor in that it conducts electricity to only a certain extent. If you make the proper connections to the doped silicon, you make it conduct electricity in one direction but not another (within a certain voltage range). Now you have a switch. It will cycle between "off" and "on" at very high rates of speed: just what you need to transmit data in the "0" and "1" form a computer requires, for example. If you connect wires to the proper voltages in the outside world from the three prime areas of the transistor, called the emitter, base, and collector, a small current caused to flow between the emitter and the base produces/controls a larger current flowing between the emitter and collector. Now you have an amplifier, which can easily be turned into an oscillator with adjustments to the outside circuitry. In essence the transistor can do anything a vacuum tube can do, and do it in a much smaller and lighter package that consumes/produces relatively little heat and is ready to go the instant it is turned on (there is no filament to warm up). Groups of transistors properly connected together with various circuit elements will perform any electric/electronic function required in telephones, radios, computers, and other such items.

The transistor led directly to the integrated circuit, developed circa 1958, where transistors and their interconnecting circuitry were chemically deposited on a silicon "chip," leading to another order-of-magnitude reduction in size, cost, and power consumption, while permitting a great increase in reliability and the speed at which electric circuits can operate. Integrated circuits became widespread in the 1960s, and the next step was to put thousands of transistors and their interconnections on a single chip. The microprocessor, a "computer on a chip," appeared in the 1970s, and many people active in the field call the microprocessor the single most important development in the world of electronics in the second half of the twentieth century. (Since the transistor was technically invented in the first half of the century, the microprocessor probably does stand out on its own.) The microprocessor led to the personal computer in the 1970s and 1980s, and all that followed, including the Internet.

To demonstrate how rapidly the state of the art grew, the first microprocessor built by a company called Intel (circa 1971) had 2,250 transistors on a chip. Gordon Moore, a key founder of Intel, observed in 1965 that the number of transistors on a chip would double every year. The press called this "Moore's Law," and although any scientist will tell you an "exponential" increase (e.g., such as the quantity of an item doubling every year) of anything can not go on forever or it would eventually fill the universe, Intel's researchers have taken a vow to keep breaking down barriers to Moore's Law. Of course they are meeting their goal by essentially shrinking the elements of the manufacturing process, but Moore's Law still operates today with a slight modification: doubling is now taking place every one and one-half or two years rather than every year. Still, in accordance with the incredible growth predicted by any exponential law, Intel grew from its 2,250 transistors per chip mark in 1971 to a truly incredible 42 *million* transistors per chip in 2000. They hope to continue their approximate doubling "every few years" through the end of the first decade of the new century.

It is this kind of technical process in manufacturing that has produced the seemingly endless proliferation of new, more powerful (and cheaper) computers, cell phones, satellites, and other components that have permitted the world to indulge in more and more personal communications at very long distances. This is the underlying basis for our great improvements in communications in the past half-century. Now that we understand the base on which we have been continuing to build, we can discuss briefly some notable items which, after their birth, caused dramatic changes in the way we communicate. This includes communication satellites, fiber-optic cables, cell phones, personal computers, and the Internet.

Satellite Communications

Broadcast waves at radio frequencies will "bounce" between the earth and the atmosphere, and thus they can be received at distances ranging up to thousands of miles. Radiotelegraphy can be conducted at such distances, but radio programming for receivers at home can be done reliably over only several hundred miles. Otherwise, direct connections via wires have to be used. Even more limiting, higher-frequency television signals can be broadcast only about 100 miles to the horizon (which is why television broadcast towers are located as high as possible, such as on top of the Empire State Building). Television waves will go on into space, and the only way to have coverage over wide areas is to use direct connections via coaxial cable to a series of relay stations. So, to have radio and television broadcasting over wide areas, some form of intervening cables and/or wires have to be used. Up to about 1960 transatlantic telephone calls were greatly limited due to a lack of available channels even on the new transatlantic cables, and live television was impossible. A relay station several hundred miles high could solve these problems. Enter, satellites.

Arthur C. Clarke, then a junior officer in the British Royal Air Force, is credited with being the first person to express the concept of communications satellites. Clarke wrote an article published in the magazine *Wireless World* in October 1945. The article was titled "Extra-Terrestrial Relays: Can Rocket Station Give World-Wide Radio Coverage?" Clarke envisioned stations manned by men circling the earth in just the proper orbit to act as a passive reflector to relay signals around the world. He was wrong in thinking that a manned station would be required to fulfill his vision, although men would be in orbit by 1961, and he was wrong in assuming the satellites would be essentially passive reflectors (rather than "active" satellites that would amplify and otherwise change the signals received), but in the particulars of the concept and the orbit required he was right on.

Any satellite, including the moon or those launched as "artificial" satellites, stays in orbit when a balance is reached between the speed of the satellite, which tends to send it flying off into space, and the pull of gravity of the earth, which tends to pull the satellite down towards the earth. When this balance is reached, the satellite stays in orbit indefinitely as it essentially keeps "falling" around the earth. If the satellite is in such a low orbit (below about 150 miles) that it encounters remnants of the earth's atmosphere, its speed is slowly reduced and it eventually falls into the earth's atmosphere and burns up. Without taking into account the effects of the atmosphere, the "orbital velocity" of a satellite, i.e. the velocity that just balances the pull of gravity, is higher the closer the satellite is to earth because the pull of gravity is stronger closer to the earth.

The moon, 240,000 miles from earth, stays in orbit at a speed of 2,300 miles per hour. At that speed, it takes 27.3 days to circle the earth. A satellite about 200 miles up would require an orbital speed of about 17,000 miles per hour, and at this speed would circle the earth in only about 90 minutes. Thus it would pass overhead about 16 times a day. In between these two extremes is a place about 22,300 miles up, which requires an orbital speed of about 7,000 miles per hour. At this speed the satellite requires 24 hours to circle the earth. But since the earth rotates in 24 hours, the satellite would appear to stay in one spot above the earth, even though it is moving at 7,000 miles per hour. This particular orbit is called a geosynchronous orbit, meaning that satellites in this orbit are in synch with the rotation of the earth. It is also called a geostationary orbit because a satellite in this orbit seems to be motionless against the background of the stars.

This is the orbit that Arthur C. Clarke was discussing in his article. Three satellites properly spaced in such an orbit would provide radio coverage for the full earth. Thus, a single satellite properly located above the United States would cover the entire country and some other areas as well. Clarke at that time never dreamed of the complexities that could be built into a satellite with the coming of the semiconductor age, so he assumed the satellites would have to be manned. But communications systems have evolved and can perform complex functions to suit most any need.

Over 5,000 satellites have been launched since the Soviet Union sent Sputnik I into orbit on October 4, 1957. Explorer I, the first United States satellite to be sent into orbit, was launched about four months later on January 31, 1958. Both satellites were launched as part of the International Geophysical Year (IGY) of 1957-58, but the immediate pressures behind their launches were military. Both nations realized space was the ultimate "high ground," and at the beginning of the "space race" the adversaries were considered balanced because the Soviet Union had more powerful rockets that could launch heavier and thus larger satellites into orbit, but the United States was considered to have more electronics expertise and thus could do more with smaller satellites. The space race essentially ended in 1969 when the United States placed men on the moon, and there was no response from the Soviet Union. But by then satellite launchings had become routine, and satellites were performing many useful services.

Satellites are used for military reconnaissance, weather forecasting, determining the location of ships and people on the earth, scientific and astronomical research, and both military and civilian communications. But by far the greatest use of those 5,000 satellites is for global communications of all kinds. The first fully successful "active" satellite built for the function of global communications was Telstar I, built by Bell Laboratories of AT&T during 1961 and launched on July 10, 1962. After that date, radio and television signals originally broadcast from stations in one country to receivers in the same or nearby countries could now be broadcast from any country to the satellite and sent (later in some cases) to receiving stations anywhere on earth. A new age of communications had arrived, even though Telstar would stay operational for only four months.

There was concern that if a huge company such as AT&T continued to put up satellites they would soon have a monopoly on satellite communications. In 1958, the United States had created the National Aeronautical and Space Administration (NASA). It was a government agency but one which was not committed to the military. Its job was to manage the research of flight both within and outside the earth's atmosphere. NASA launched the first two AT&T satellites for a fee (Telstar was originally planned to encompass 50-100 satellites and a number of ground stations because at only 500 miles up the satellite was "in view" of a given fixed transmitter for only a few minutes and many satellites would be required to be sure one was always in view), but NASA then went looking for more players to get into the satellite communications game. The next quantum leap in satellite communications was the Syncom satellite built by the then–Hughes Aircraft Company in 1961-62 and launched in 1963. As noted, Telstar was in an orbit only about 500 miles up, and some other satellites were also launched into similar orbits. But Hughes was proposing to launch a satellite into an orbit 22,300 miles up, the geosynchronous orbit proposed by Arthur C. Clarke in his 1945 article. It would be "in view" 24 hours a day. If the Hughes satellite succeeded, it would instantly make the prior satellites obsolete from a communications standpoint.

There were many technical difficulties to overcome to build a satellite that could operate at such a distance, and many people in the field were skeptical of the satellite proposed by Hughes, including some higher levels of Hughes management. But the three key Hughes engineers, Harold Rosen, Don Williams, and Tom Hudspeth, were so sure they could do it, that each wrote a personal check for $10,000 in February 1960 to continue to fund their work at Hughes. The next month a decision was made by Hughes management to fund the work without the individual contributions of their engineers. However, there were also many political problems to overcome.

The Army was proposing to build what was being called the "24 hour satellite," and they supposedly had the charter to do so, rather than NASA. However, the Army satellite, called Advent, would be much larger (and heavier to launch) than the Hughes design because the Army proposed to use a three-axis stabilization system, while Hughes was going to achieve stabilization in orbit by simply making the satellite spin like a top. After much discussion during the rest of 1960 and early 1961, NASA took over the responsibility for building the 24- hour satellite and awarded a contract to Hughes on August 11, 1961, to build three 24-hour satellites that would be known as Syncom I, II, and III.

Syncom I was launched February 14, 1963, but it worked for only a few minutes before being lost when it was being injected into its final orbit. However, the second Syncom was launched five months later on July 26, 1963, and successfully reached its final orbit, giving instantaneous coverage between the United States and countries across the Atlantic Ocean. Syncom III was launched just one month before the 1964 Olympics in Tokyo, and it provided coverage of the Pacific Ocean. Accordingly, two-thirds of the world got to see live action from the games.

The success of the Hughes satellites ended the debate between proponents of a fleet of "medium altitude" communications satellites (MACS) and those of geosynchronous 24-hour satellites that were permanently in view. The geosynchronous satellite was the choice. To regulate the new satellite business, the Communications Satellite Company (Comsat) was created when President Kennedy signed the Communications Satellite Act in 1962. Comsat would use private companies to produce satellites, but Comsat would own the satellite systems after they were built. It would, however, have to sell its satellite services through private companies. In a classic attempt to "have your cake and eat it too," Comsat would insure government control in the critical communications satellite business, but it would also ensure that private companies had a piece of the action. The arrangement worked very well, with military requirements being met by separate contracts between the military and private companies.

In 1964, a group of 18 nations formed a worldwide satellite network to regulate the industry and to offer satellite services to countries that wished to rent them rather than build their own satellites. This group was called the International Telecommunications Satellite Organization or Intelsat. Comsat was the representative of the United States at Intelsat, and at the beginning also offered management services to Intelsat to build satellites for use by the international group. In an example of how the organizations would work together, Comsat contracted with Hughes Aircraft to build a satellite called Early Bird (later called Intelsat 1), and contracted with NASA to launch it. Early Bird was launched April 6, 1965, and it transmitted to earth stations in the United States, England, France, and Germany. An earth station is a very large (and thus very sensitive) station that "talks" to an international satellite and then sends transmissions to the rest of the country via conventional ground-based means.

Early Bird was the first of many such successful operations launched by Intelsat during the rest of the century. By 2000, Intelsat was generating $1.1 billion in revenues and had over 143 members serving over 180 countries. Comsat, however, was no longer the only way in the United States to deal with Intelsat (and also with Inmarsat, which provided mobile satellite communications worldwide). Showing how satellite communications had essentially become a routine fact of life, Comsat had been acquired in September 1999 by a private company, the Lockheed Martin Corporation, although it took until late in 2000 to gain all of the Congressional approvals involved. As part of the acquisition, Congress ended Comsat's exclusive right to deal with Intelsat in February 2000. Both Intelsat and Inmarsat have become fully privatized companies, and Lockheed is a big shareholder in each. Ironically, Comsat is now involved in providing networking, data processing, and other services in addition to its remaining satellite business, but Lockheed sees satellites as the slowest growing part of Comsat's many business areas. As in many other areas of communication, the business has become a very big business, but many of the players have changed.

Fiber Optics

Another technology change that has affected the once-incredible growth of the satellite communications business is the growth of the fiber-optics business. "Conducting" light through tubes or streams of water for decorative purposes has been done since the 1800s, but it wasn't until development of the laser in the 1960s and low-loss optical fibers in the 1970s that the combination could be considered for communication purposes. A laser generates light that is at only one frequency and is in phase. Ordinary light is a combination of frequencies (different colors) that are out of phase with each other.

This one-frequency in-phase characteristic of the laser is what permits it to be used in medical applications when the power is appropriately high. The high operating frequency of a laser is attractive for communications applications because the amount of information a transmitted wave can carry (bandwidth) is proportional to the frequency of the wave, and the laser's light has an operating frequency that is several orders of magnitude higher than even the operating frequency of satellites, which are already hundreds of times higher than ordinary radio and television broadcasts.

By the 1970s optical fibers to carry the laser light with low loss had been developed. An optical fiber is a very clear flexible tube of glass that is thinner than an eyelash. Such fibers can be built in sections up to six miles long. AT&T installed the first optical fibers in Chicago in 1977 after much development work by Bell Laboratories on semiconductor lasers and the Corning Glass Company and DuPont on fiber-optics. In 1988, AT&T laid the first fiber-optic cable under the Atlantic Ocean. Fiber-optic cables have since criss-crossed the world. Repeaters to boost the signal had to be installed only every six miles in fiber-optics as opposed to every mile in copper cables in routine use. Recent advances in technology have pushed the distance light can travel in a fiber-optic cable to over 500 miles while carrying six hundred thousand phone calls at once under the Pacific Ocean. Use of very high frequencies and special cables may eliminate the need for repeaters.

Thus fiber-optic cables can outdo satellites in terms of the information they can carry and they also offer high speed. Although they require some amount of infrastructure, the total costs are becoming cheaper than the costs of building and launching satellites. Also, fiber-optic cables have longer lives than satellites. Each type of communication system offers a combination of advantages and disadvantages, but the use of fiber-optic cables is growing fast and will displace satellites in many applications.

Cell Phones and LEOs

Another new technology that competes with other communication systems but may simultaneously increase the use of satellite systems is the cellular telephone, called simply the "cell phone." Basic "mobile" phones have been around for many decades, but they were generally bulky devices and needed to be somewhere near a transmitting station to be used. Then the "cellular" system was developed in the 1970s. Towers that receive and transmit telephone messages were built across the country. As someone traveled in his or her car, the signal was automatically switched to a new "cell" or tower. The towers communicated by standard broadcast waves to accompany the caller across the country. The cellular phone was born.

The next improvement was the almost-obvious step of having mobile telephones talk to satellites intended for that purpose. The ongoing miracles of semiconductor manufacturing brought the size of the mobile telephone down to something that could be slipped into a shirt pocket. Such phones are more like tiny computers/radios than telephones. This application brought back the old low- and medium-altitude satellites (usually using orbits from 500 to a few thousand miles high) that had been displaced by the geostationary satellite (with an orbit of 22,300 miles) in the 1960s. The new satellites are called LEOS, for low-earth-orbit satellites. They are designed to focus on a single task, such as providing cellular phone service. That means they are less complex and much cheaper than a multiple-task satellite. Improvements in technology since the 1960s make it possible to launch low-orbit satellites while avoiding the radiation belts that surround the lower reaches of the earth's atmosphere. The LEO is easier for signals to reach in its relatively low orbit, and it is less expensive to launch. In fact, several LEOs can be launched at once using the same rocket. A fleet of them is still required to be sure one is always in view, but essentially a fleet of 20–30 LEOs can be built, launched, and operated for less money than it would cost to build, launch, and operate a system of three geostationary satellites. Also, a group of LEOs can be placed over any desired point on earth whereas a geostationary satellite must be near the equator.

But however many advantages LEOs seem to have, the law of supply and demand still applies whether one is selling cheese or satellite services. The cautionary tale of the Iridium system is an excellent example of this problem. The Motorola Company made a $5 billion investment in a plan to build and launch as many as 77 satellites (Iridium is number 77 on the periodic table of the elements, hence the name of the system), in an orbit height of about 500 miles, to use in a cellular phone system. However, the mobile phones to connect with the system were a failure even though they cost about $3,000 each. Many critics called them a "brick," saying that they were as heavy and bulky to carry around as a brick would be, and they also worked as well as a brick would. There were few takers who were willing to pay $7 a minute to make calls on the system.

Motorola unfortunately chose the end of the 1990s to build the system. At that time, continued launches had created an over-capacity problem throughout the mid–1990s into the late 1990s. By some estimates nearly 40 percent of the capacity of all the satellite systems was not being used. Iridium filed for bankruptcy protection in the spring of 2000, about a year after it opened for business. No buyers materialized, and a decision was made to let the 66 operating satellites and eight spares fall from orbit and burn up in the earth's atmosphere to save the costs of continuing to operate the system. At the last minute a buyer offered about $25 million for the system that took at least $5 billion to build. The bankruptcy judge accepted the offer as the best that was available, and the new owner took over in December 2000. As one observer noted, that was about one-half cent on the dollar: like buying a $150,000 Porsche 911 for $750. At the time there were other bankrupt systems around that had suffered from the same over-capacity problem as Iridium.

Everything changed about nine months later with the horrendous events of September 11, 2001, and the deadly destruction in New York and at the Pentagon. Suddenly there was a war in Afghanistan and afterwards in Iraq. The military needed field communication systems in countries that had no infrastructure to support telephone calls and other information exchanges between commanders and troops in the field and between the troops themselves. The Iridium system is now about to make a profit. With very low debt and greatly expanded military contracts, the company has brought the cost of handsets down to $1,500 from $3,000, and the cost of calls is down to $1.50 a minute from $7 a minute.

Other LEO companies have emerged from bankruptcy to try to follow Iridium's example in making a profit with greatly lowered operating costs and greatly increased revenue from the military and other agencies involved with "homeland security." Motorola can only think of what might have been. The old saying that "timing is everything" has never been truer, and the importance of communications technology in addressing the needs of the country has also never been more evident.

Speaking of timing, it is interesting to note that the desire for "wireless" communications has never been higher. The new term "Wi-Fi" has become a part of the language. The term specifically means "Wireless Fidelity," but it has become a catchall phrase meaning that individuals want to be able to communicate with any other individuals by clicking on their cell phone or personal computer or similar electronic marvel and begin speaking. They don't want to be required to "plug-in" to some communication port, to be within some specific distance of some transmission tower, or to have any other requirement that they would interpret as limiting their ability to communicate now.

"Wireless" communication began with Marconi circa 1900 as the only way to communicate over the oceans or the vast areas of empty space on earth. Radio and television seized the technique to communicate over wide areas, but telephone lines and coaxial cable were widely used to supplement "broadcasting." When satellites were developed, "wireless" techniques were the only way to contact them, but fiber-optic cables laid by the hundreds under the sea (to supplement those on land) began to become competitive. Now, however, people demand individual "wireless" connections, regardless of the fact that various earth-bound cables may be used to carry these "wireless" contacts part of the way on their journey. A significant part of new technology development in tiny antennas, receivers, and transmitters is now directed towards this desire for immediate personal "wireless" communication.

Personal Computers

The personal computer was not originally developed as a communication device, but it has become one of the most valuable communication tools we have. The first electronic computer built in the United States was completed at the University of Pennsylvania in 1946. It was built under contract to the military, and its prime intended use was calculating the "orbit" of artillery shells so that range corrections could be made in firing the shells in war. The final computer took up several rooms on one floor of a building, contained 18,000 vacuum tubes, and weighed about 30 tons. The semiconductor manufacturing process has since brought the computer down to laptop size, and that much-smaller computer has almost infinitely more calculating power and versatility than its monstrous predecessor of 1946.

This great reduction in size and power consumption has made computers ubiquitous in communication equipment of all types. It was only after the development of the microprocessor in 1971 by Intel that people begin to think seriously about putting a "small" computer on workplace desktops and in homes. The "small" was in terms of computing power as compared to a mainframe computer, not the physical size. By 1977, Steve Jobs and Steve Wozniak were building the Apple II computer intended for personal use. Their company had literally started in a garage. The great success of Apple brought huge International Business Machines (IBM) into the personal-computer business in 1981, and IBM soon took over the top spot in the industry. IBM also must be credited with contracting with an obscure company named Microsoft to develop a software operating system for its personal computers, and for making an Intel microprocessor the "standard" semiconductor for the operation of its computers. Hundreds of companies jumped into the personal computer business to make "clones" of the basic IBM computer, i.e. computers that contained the Microsoft operating system and the latest Intel microprocessor. These clones would run the same programs as the IBM machine, but were cheaper. IBM eventually became just another entrant in the personal-computer field, but Microsoft grew into the dominant software company in the world, and Intel grew into the dominant semiconductor company in the world. Both companies now have annual revenues near $40 billion. The "leaders" of the personal computer market now are really Microsoft and Intel, although neither company wants to be in the hardware end of the business.

One of the primary "clone" companies in the early 1980s was Compaq Computer, a company founded in 1981 just after IBM introduced its first personal computer. Compaq set a record with sales of $111 million in its first full year of business (1983), and it created an historical turning point in the computer industry in 1986 when it introduced a new computer based on Intel's "386" chip before IBM did so. The other clone manufacturers then copied Compaq instead of IBM. Personal computers became like a commodity with price being the determinant factor. Compaq eventually rose to the top of the personal computer hardware business in the United States. Also, in this environment, a company later called simply Dell Computer, which had been started by Michael Dell in his college dormitory room, became a key factor in the industry by selling clones via mail order at very low prices. Dell sold $70 million worth of personal computers in 1986, increased it to over $150 million the next year, and eventually rose to be the number-two hardware supplier in the new century behind Compaq.

By 2001, with Dell closing on Compaq, Hewlett-Packard and Compaq merged to become the second-biggest computer and office machine company in the United States behind IBM. In the personal computer sector, the newly merged company and Dell now split about a third of the market, with Dell having a slight edge. But the two top companies are far ahead of the rest of the personal computer hardware companies. IBM leads the host of companies making up the other two-thirds of the market, with IBM holding about a 5 percent share.

But this is only background to our prime story of the use of personal computers in the business of communication. The development of the Internet (as discussed in the following section) made it possible to interconnect computers in a way that permits them to "talk" to each other, exchanging e-mail, data, and nearly any piece of information the computer can process. In homes with both computers and a connection to the Internet, the computer is now the prime element for communication, not the telephone. It is estimated that two out of every three people in the United States over the age of three now use computers. Total computer sales in units in the world as of today exceed one billion. In the next 50 years it is forecast that more computers will have been sold than there are people in the world. Soon there will be very few homes that do not have access to a computer. In the United States, about 175 million people or nearly 60 percent of the population can now access the Internet from their homes. The combination of a computer and access to the Internet will eventually make the computer the prime element for communication in nearly every home.

This is a good place to point out how the electronic computer has grown in terms of becoming an everyday tool compared to its unique status when it was first developed. Around 1950, when the first electronic computer had been developed at the University of Pennsylvania, and other computers were in the works, a forecast was made of the potential computer market, and the conclusion was that the total worldwide market for computers might be as high as 150 units. This followed a 1943 forecast by Thomas Watson, the revered chairman of mighty IBM, that "there is a world market for maybe five computers." These forecasts now seem ridiculous in view of the one billion units of all kinds that have been sold to date, but it must be mentioned that these forecasts were for the very large units being built at the time. Even though the transistor had just been invented before the latter forecast, no one could imagine the emergence of the semiconductor manufacturing process, or the microprocessor, or the idea of making computers for personal use in the home.

Similarly, circa 1900, a telephone salesman trying to get an order from a business manager was rebuffed with the statement "We don't need any telephones, we already have one." Once again, no one at the time could imagine the growth in telephone usage. Large hotels in New York, instead of employing messengers to crowd the stairways and elevators of the building answering message signals, installed telephones instead. By 1904, the Waldorf-Astoria hotel had 1,120 telephones, the most under one roof in the world at the time. By 1909, the 100 largest hotels in New York had 21,000 telephones, as many as were in the entire continent of Africa in that year. Today, a household with fewer than several telephones scattered around the house is unusual, and the number of subscribers to cellular phones, now more like tiny computers and radios than telephones, exceeds the total number of subscribers to telephones connected by wires. There are about 1.14 billion subscribers to cell phones in the world, approximately one out of every six people, led by over 140 million subscribers in the United States.

The human urge to communicate grows ever stronger, and it has found a new way to express itself in the personal computer and the Internet.

The Internet

No one set out to invent the Internet in the way men set out to invent the telegraph or the telephone. The Internet simply grew and evolved in an iterative process as the computer, especially the personal computer, grew and evolved. Looking back, key steps in the process can be identified, but they are identifiable mainly in retrospect, not as part of a great overall plan. The evolutionary nature of the Internet still continues today.

The Internet owes its start, as do so many other developments in the field of electronic communications, to the military. In the 1950s and 1960s many experiments in communications networks were undertaken by and on behalf of the military with the objective of finding ways to make it possible for such networks to survive hostile nuclear attacks. Out of these efforts evolved the so-called ARPANET in 1969, an experimental four-computer network put together by the Advanced Research Projects Agency (ARPA). This was an attempt to make it possible for research scientists to communicate and to make maximum use of their computer resources, which ARPA was generally paying for. Scientists would have to show they were making maximum use of the net before they could buy new (generally large and powerful) computers.

By 1971, ARPANET linked about 24 computers (called "hosts") at 15 different sites, including MIT, Harvard, and some equally prestigious West Coast schools. This climbed rapidly to over 200 hosts by 1981, just as personal computers were beginning to flood the marketplace. In 1983, the military portion of the ARPANET was moved to the MILNET, and the ARPANET was abandoned by 1990. However, in the late 1980s, the National Science Foundation had put together its own NSFNET, and permitted everyone access to it, although most of the users were computer science students and their professors. In a critical step, users were given a chance to develop applications and to have a say in how the net was operated.

In 1988, a "chat" application was developed which gained worldwide attention as a way to get news about the 1991 Persian Gulf War. During 1989 and 1990, Tim Berners-Lee of Great Britain developed what became known as the World Wide Web while he was working at the Center for Nuclear Research (CERN) in Switzerland. Legislation in the United States in the early 1990s supported the Internet concept, and changed the National Science Foundation net to the NREN (National Research and Educational Network). The first "browser" for accessing the Internet came out in 1991, and by 1998 a software company called Netscape was locked in battle with Microsoft and its Explorer for the top spot for software to access the Internet, but after an antitrust wrangle (which still goes on in some states), Microsoft emerged triumphant with about 95 percent of the business.

As new applications have been added to the Internet, it has become popular with users for the exchange of "e-mail," "chat rooms," and "instant messaging" between parties located literally anywhere in the world. Now immense amounts of information can be found about nearly any subject, just as if the Internet were a collection of all the reference books in the world. It has also become popular as a place to buy (or sell) just about anything. In the second quarter of 2002, U.S. customers spent a record $17.5 billion via the Internet, and the number continues to grow.

As noted, the Internet is not owned by anybody, except perhaps its users, and it essentially "just grew" as outlined above. In 1994, a total of 3 million people made use of the Internet, most of who were in the United

States. In early 2002, 160 million Americans had access to the Internet, followed by the Chinese with 56 million people. English was the "native" language used by about 40 percent of the roughly 560 million people in the world who were now online. It has truly become the world's most significant communication tool. Perhaps surprisingly, a survey found that American mothers averaged about one-third more time online per week than American teenagers.

A "domain" is the fundamental part of an address on the Internet. Since 1998, the system of assigning domain names has been overseen by a non-profit corporation called the Internet Corporation for Assigned Names and Numbers (ICANN). It is estimated that the number of Internet "domain" names that have been registered has grown from 627,000 in 1996 to more than 30 million by mid–2002. It is notable that all of these Internet functions are performed by voluntary organizations whose main interest is keeping the Internet functioning in an orderly fashion. The Internet has no CEO, and is not owned or funded by any one institution, organization, or government. Its development is guided by the Internet Society (ISOC), fully composed of volunteers. The ISOC appoints the Internet Architectural Board (IAB) which works on issues of standards, network resources, etc.

The Internet is truly an international development, and it has grown primarily because so many of its functions are performed by people who are most interested in keeping the medium open to everyone, rather than people who are looking to make some sort of profit. As noted before, the prime access to the Internet is the personal computer, and this makes the personal computer the most important communication tool in the world. Both the Internet and the personal computer continue to be improved by dramatic inventions taking place on a routine basis in the field of semiconductor manufacturing. It is very hard to predict the future of these two elements, except to say that there doesn't appear to be any limit whatsoever to the urge of people to communicate with each other.

Summary

In summary, the history of communication in the United States is linked to the ongoing development of electronics in the United States. The country started out with the usual communication tools of speech and writing. The telegraph, which is now a part of history more than an active part of the present, was the first milestone in moving from conventional communication forms to electronic communication. It is almost a direct line from the telegraph to the telephone, and thence to movies, phonograph records, and radio and television broadcasting. The invention of the transistor in 1948, and the development of semiconductor manufacturing that followed, paved the way for new communication tools such as satellites, fiber-optics, cell phones and LEOS, the personal computer, and the Internet. As is the case in so many developments in the history of the United States, more dramatic achievements have been made in the past 50 years than were made in the first 200 years of the country. This follows the worldwide trend in nearly all areas of technology, in that more achievements have been made in the last 150 years than in the previous 2,000 years, or even in the whole 10,000 years of human civilization.

CHRONOLOGY OF COMMUNICATION

Our chronology of communication in the United States commences with the establishment of the first post office systems in the colonies, and the beginning of newspaper publishing. Then we will track the various publications that influenced the beginning and outcome of the Revolutionary War, and the pressures for more rapid communication and for communication at a distance that led to the development of the telegraph. The telegraph was the true turning point in communications in the United States (and the world) that led to the immense variety of electronic-based communications we enjoy today.

January 22, 1673—This was the inaugural trip in a monthly postal service between New York and Boston. This was the beginning of official postal service in the colonies, even though it was done without the blessing of anyone back in England.

September 25, 1690—The first newspaper was published in the American colonies, but it was banned after its first and only day of publication. It was called *Public Occurrences, Both Foreign and Domestic,* and was published in Boston by Benjamin Harris. The local (British) administration was outraged that Harris had failed to get prior approval and/or a license from those appointed to grant one, and the newspaper was closed after one day. It would be 14 years before anyone would again try to publish a newspaper.

February 17, 1691—The postmaster general in England approved a postmaster general for the American colonies. It would take more than a year for someone to fill the post, but not only would this give official blessing to the postal system in the colonies, it would eventually embolden some local postmasters general to go into the newspaper-publishing business.

April 17, 1704 — A bookseller who had been appointed postmaster general of Boston, John Campbell, published the second newspaper in the colonies. It was called the *Boston News-Letter*. It never was very prosperous, but it kept publishing against competition from subsequent postmasters general of Boston who decided to enter the field.

August 19, 1721 — The third newspaper published in Boston and the fourth in the colonies, the *New England Courant*, made its debut on this date. It marked the entrance of a young Benjamin Franklin into the newspaper-publishing business. The *Courant* was originally published by James Franklin, Ben Franklin's older half-brother, who had gained experience earlier from printing the second newspaper to appear in Boston. James Franklin was imprisoned for criticizing the government for failing to crack down on pirates harassing local shipping off the New England coast. As a result, 13-year-old Ben Franklin, who had been apprenticed to his half-brother as a way of escaping his father's tallow shop, assumed the responsibility of setting type, printing and delivering the newspaper. When the older James Franklin was ordered six months later not to publish any more newspapers, Ben Franklin's name appeared on the masthead as editor and publisher. The younger Franklin's name stayed on the masthead until 1726, even though he had departed in 1723. Ben disliked his older brother and left as soon as his apprenticeship was up.

September 25, 1729 — This date marked the first issue of the *Pennsylvania Gazette*, published in Philadelphia by Benjamin Franklin and his partner, Hugh Meredith. It was essentially the seventh newspaper published in the colonies as Franklin and his partner bought the existing seventh newspaper and modified its name. Franklin had traveled from Boston to New York and on to Philadelphia to work as a printer, took two years off to travel to London, and then returned for good to Philadelphia.

By 1730 Franklin was sole owner of the newspaper, which he made a great success. He then published the *General Magazine*, and in 1732 he started his famous *Poor Richard's Almanac* which ran for 25 years to 1757. Franklin became famous in the colonies and on the Continent for his many inventions, his civic services, and his writings, but in terms of communications one of his next important steps was to write letters of introduction for a young Englishman, Tom Paine, in 1774.

January 9, 1776— A pamphlet entitled *Common Sense*, written by Englishman Tom Paine (whose name as author was not revealed until later), was published in Philadelphia. The pamphlet urged Americans to declare independence from the "unlawful" monarchy in Britain. In a short time, more than 100,000 copies were in circulation, and the pamphlet had a great effect on the members of the Continental Congress who were gathering in Philadelphia. Paine would later write a series of 16 pamphlets called *The American Crisis*, starting in December 1776 and continuing through the official end of the war in 1783, encouraging Americans in their battle with Britain.

July 3, 1776— The Continental Congress spent the day in debate over the Declaration of Independence. Thomas Jefferson had written it during the previous month, with advice from Benjamin Franklin and John Adams. The Congress had voted to declare independence the previous day, and Jefferson's document was the written vehicle through which the declaration would be made. Following a day of some alterations, the document was finally agreed to, and it was officially signed on July 4, 1776. The United States had been born. The eloquence of Jefferson's words would eventually trigger similar revolutions in other countries.

January 14, 1790— The secretary of the treasury of the new United States, Alexander Hamilton, made a proposal to redeem all of the paper money and scrip issued by the Continental Congress during the Revolutionary War. In addition, he proposed that the new federal government assume all the debts of the states. This would give greater credibility to the states and the federal government in their dealings with foreign countries. It was finally agreed to do so, but the selling of $80 million in bonds would be required to finance the operation. The marketing of this immense (for the times) sum led to the creation of the New York Stock Exchange (NYSE). The normal operation of the NYSE brought immense pressure to bear on the need for improved communications between the world at large and the NYSE and the NYSE and other exchanges. Greater speed was needed to get the information to the NYSE no matter where the information originated.

One system using flagmen, telescopes, and semaphore signals on tall buildings located every 6–8 miles between the NYSE and the Philadelphia Stock Exchange was able to cover the 90 miles between the cities in about 30 minutes, but it was not as useful in bad weather. Pressure continued to build for better methods of communication.

June 18, 1812— The United States declared war on England. The last battle of this war was the battle of New Orleans in 1815. The United States won a great victory, with over 1,000 men (mostly British) being killed or wounded.

The battle actually took place two weeks after peace was declared. This event added more urgency to the need for improved communications that would travel at very high speed over long distances.

Fall 1832—An American named Samuel F. B. Morse, a well-known portrait painter and a founder of the National Academy of Design in 1825, was returning from a second trip to study art in England when another passenger described to him experiments in Europe with electromagnetism. Morse was an amateur scientist and had studied electricity. The talk triggered a dream in which Morse saw wires carrying messages around the world, and he determined to develop the electromagnetic telegraph. He also developed a code, now known as Morse code, to be used with his system, but it did not differ greatly from similar code systems in use in Europe in semaphore applications.

The word telegraph derives from Greek roots, with "tele" meaning "far" and "graph" meaning "writing." The word had previously been applied to systems using flags or smoke signals or flashes of light, and a system based on light was called an "optical telegraph" in 1791 in France. The United States had offered a prize of $30,000 for a workable proposal for some such system to operate along the east coast of the United States. Morse was determined to develop a system based on the use of electricity. Many other scientists in Europe were already working on such systems, but no one had yet demonstrated an operating system. The work of the famous American scientist Joseph Henry, and of men named Alfred Vail and Leonard Gale, are credited with helping Morse perfect his telegraph. Vail and Gale became partners in the project, although Morse was finally credited alone as the prime developer.

September 3, 1833—The *New York Sun* began the era of the "penny press" on this date by offering its newspapers for sale for a penny. The significance of the penny press was not its price; the name simply was used to refer to newspapers that were written to appeal to mass audiences. Newspapers had previously been written mainly for upper-class readers and sold primarily through subscription lists sometimes as small as a few hundred readers. Increased general education and the concentration of the population in the cities led to the concept of the "penny press": the paper's content was greatly broadened, and it was sold in the streets for one penny rather than primarily by subscription.

This led the next day (September 4, 1833) to an advertisement in the *Sun* appealing to unemployed men to consider selling the paper in the streets. They could buy at a discount and realize a profit from selling at full price. This advertisement resulted in the first paperboy, a ten-year-old who answered the advertisement. The penny press was a huge success, and the papers sold in the thousands, then the hundred of thousands, and into the millions by the end of the century. This helped establish the concept of a mass audience for the movies, phonographs, radios, and televisions that were to follow at the end of the nineteenth century and on into the 20th century.

September 28, 1837— Morse filed a caveat for a patent on his model of the telegraph. A caveat is essentially only a notice of an intention to file a patent, but it establishes a date that is useful if court action becomes necessary to establish priority in patent filings. This did happen in Morse's case, but he finally prevailed: he officially received a patent in 1840. Some references credit this date in 1837 as marking the invention of the telegraph, but a workable system demonstrating the commercial use of the telegraph in the field had yet to be developed.

February 21, 1838— Morse demonstrated an operating electrical telegraph system to President Martin Van Buren and his cabinet in Washington, D.C. However, he was unable to convince them to put up the $30,000 prize money for a field trial of the system, which would require funds in advance to build a test line and operate it. The so-called financial panic of 1837 had made money tight, and Morse could not get a commitment.

Morse later tried to find potential investors in England, France, and Russia while he was traveling there to get patent protections. There were no takers, but Morse was convinced that his version of the telegraph was superior to those he saw abroad. Finally, Morse got the grant of $30,000 from Congress on March 3, 1843. He made plans to build a demonstration line between Washington and Baltimore.

May 24, 1844— The first "commercial" electric telegraph message in history, "What hath God wrought?," was sent over a 40-mile line from Washington to Baltimore on this date, and then transmitted back to show it had been properly received. The message was selected from the Bible by the daughter of the commissioner of patents.

Morse had first tried burying the telegraph wires in underground pipes, but the wires were not properly insulated and in essence the line shorted out. Running out of money and time, Morse agreed to a suggestion to have the wires put on poles and trees, using the necks of glass bottles for insulators. The system finally worked. The age of "communication at a distance" using electric means had arrived.

The United States government, not wanting to be in competition with its own post office, sold its interest in Morse's system to private investors, while retaining its right of eventual government regulation. In a few decades, a single company called Western Union dominated the field of telegraphy. Thus, the United States did not follow the lead of Great Britain and other European countries where the post office was in charge of the telegraph and all such communications systems. In retrospect, this was probably a great boon to all the inventors that followed in the field of communications in the United States. They were able to pursue their inventions outside the great bureaucracy of the government.

Telegraph lines soon sprang up all over the more heavily populated areas of the United States, and most of Europe. The telegraph was so successful that thoughts turned to trying to lay a cable under the Atlantic Ocean to connect the United States with England and Europe.

August 16, 1858— The first telegraph messages between the United States and Europe were sent between Queen Victoria and President Buchanan on this date. They used the first successful undersea telegraph cable laid by a company organized by Cyrus Field. The company had been trying since 1857 to get a cable laid, but the cables kept breaking. On the fifth try over a two-year period, a cable connecting Newfoundland and Ireland was laid without breaking on August 5, 1858. The first message was then sent on the 16th, but cable service was suspended on September 1, 1858, as the cable connection faded and failed to carry a message. The cable had remained useable only about three weeks. Field planned to reorganize and try again, but the Civil War intervened. It would not be until 1866 that Field would get to try again successfully.

April 13, 1860— A private company called the Pony Express began service on this date. The Pony Express had tried to get a contract from the government for its services, but as its idea was generally perceived as "impossible," no government contract was forthcoming until the last four months of the Pony Express's existence in 1861. The idea of the Pony Express was to carry mail by horseback, using a series of riders, between St. Joseph, Missouri, and Sacramento, California, a distance of about 2,000 miles. This was a response to the need for faster communication to California, especially after gold was discovered there in 1848. The distance involved was almost the same as the distance the cable under the Atlantic Ocean had to cover. St. Joseph was the furthest point to the west that was served by the telegraph and the railroads. The Pony Express delivered the mail in just over 10 days, about half the time stage carriers took using the southern route via Santa Fe. The Pony Express ended service on October 24, 1861, when the transcontinental telegraph line was completed. The Pony Express lasted only 18 months, but has remained a romantic story in American history ever since it was born in 1860.

October 24, 1861— The transcontinental telegraph line was completed between the east and west coasts of the United States on this date. This greatly reduced the isolation of California and helped hold the county together east and west just as it was coming apart north and south in the Civil War. The transcontinental railroad, which was built between 1863 and 1869, was required by Congress to also build a telegraph line along the railroad right of way as construction on the railroad itself took place. Communication by telegraph was no longer just a convenience but an essential part of the nation's economy.

July 27, 1866— The successful laying of a new telegraph cable under the Atlantic Ocean was completed on this day. Cyrus Field and his company had tried again in 1865, only to have the cable break when two-thirds of it had been laid by the *Great Eastern*, the largest ship in the world. Field tried again successfully in 1866, and also raised and repaired the broken cable from the previous year. Now two telegraph lines were available under the Atlantic Ocean, and both worked without fading out later. In 15 years, there would be 100,000 miles of undersea telegraph cable in the world. The first step in building a "global village" of instantaneous communication at a distance had been completed.

June 16, 1874— On this date James Clerk Maxwell, a famous Scottish physicist, officially opened the Cavendish Laboratory in England in honor of the great British physicist, Henry Cavendish. Many significant discoveries in nuclear particle physics would later be made in the laboratory Maxwell had designed and helped set up.

This was the last significant public act Maxwell would perform. His health was already declining, and he would die at the early age of 47 only five years later. Although rarely noted as such, Maxwell was really the father of the wireless communication and radio broadcasting that would begin in 20 years and carry through the twentieth century. As early as 1862, Maxwell had noted that light is simply one manifestation of the basic electromagnetic spectrum. He continued to work in this area, and during 1873, just before he finished his work on the Cavendish Laboratory, he pulled all his work together in a summary titled *A Treatise on Electricity and Magnetism*. This publication contained what are now known as Maxwell's equations, and they formed the basis for the beginning of quantum mechanics in the next century. Of greater interest to communications, this paper showed that there must be waves of electromagnetic energy, similar to light, existing throughout the measurable frequency spectrum. Once the significance of this prediction was grasped, experiments a dozen years later by Heinrich Hertz would lead to Guglielmo Marconi's experiments in 1895 and the creation of wireless communication at the end of the century.

As shown in detail in the Appendix, the lowest frequencies are perceived as radiant heat and electric power; they then go up through the range of human speech and hearing in the area of thousands of cycles per second (one thousand cycles per second is one kilocycle), proceed through radio waves up to microwaves at one thousand million cycles per second (one gigahertz), and arrive at visible light (one million gigahertz). This is about the highest frequency used in today's communications in fiber-optics. It would take an increase of about another eight orders of magnitude above light to reach the frequencies of deadly cosmic rays. The known frequency spectrum thus covers about 14 orders of magnitude above zero, but we use "only" about the first eight orders of magnitude for communicating.

Little of this was known at the time Maxwell published the summary of his work, but this summary is the bedrock on which all future communications were to rest. Looking back, it is relatively easy to see that if Maxwell's conclusions were correct, then it must be possible to send waves through the air carrying communication information without the need for wires, i.e. "wireless communication." As noted, Heinrich Hertz in 1888 proved that such waves exist, but it was not until the arrival of Guglielmo Marconi on the scene circa 1895 that practical use was made of Maxwell's theory for communications.

February 14, 1876— Alexander Graham Bell filed a patent claim on his ideas for the telephone. Bell had worked with the deaf and hearing-impaired (his mother and wife were hearing-impaired), and he was trying to improve the telegraph to get it to carry a wider range of signals as part of a device he was developing to help hearing-impaired people learn to speak. He soon realized his device could carry all the frequencies emitted by the human voice, and he knew he was on the track to a telephone rather than just an improved telegraph.

Ironically, an inventor named Elisha Gray filed a caveat on a patent for a telephone only two hours after Bell had filed. This two hours meant that eventually it was the Bell Telephone Company that later reigned supreme for some time in the field of communications, rather than the Gray telephone company.

March 7, 1876— Alexander Graham Bell was granted United States Patent 174,465 for the telephone. It is still considered the most lucrative single patent ever granted in the United States. Bell was still hard at work trying to reduce the patent to practice. He had a working receiver section, but the transmitter was still giving him problems. Because Bell was not adept with his hands, he had hired a technician named Thomas A. Watson to help him in the laboratory.

March 10, 1876—Bell, working in the laboratory on his latest telephone-transmitter idea, accidentally spilled some acid on his clothes. He called to Watson, who was three rooms down the hall at the receiving end of the telephone system. Watson clearly heard Bell's voice, coming from the telephone, saying "Mister Watson, come here. I want to see you." That sentence (or some close variation of it) was the first telephone conversation. Bell had successfully reduced his telephone concept to practice through intensive work from the day he originally filed his patent idea. Now he had his patent and a working system, but there would be much litigation to come before Bell was ruled to be the original inventor of the telephone.

May 10, 1876—Alexander Graham Bell demonstrated his telephone system at the American Academy of Arts and Sciences in Boston. The demonstration was a success, but Bell was still unable to raise enough money to begin to build a telephone system. As with the telegraph, there were substantial infrastructure costs involved—telephone poles, wires, the telephones themselves, connection devices, etc. It seemed clear that the telephone was the coming thing, but not so clear that investors were willing to risk money to launch a system.

June 25, 1876—On a hot humid Sunday in the main exhibition hall at the Philadelphia Exposition honoring the centennial of the United States, judges trying to determine the most exciting invention at the exposition witnessed a demonstration of Bell's telephone. Ultimately, the telephone won the top prize at the exposition. The publicity from this event made it much easier thereafter for Bell to raise money to develop his new invention.

July 9, 1877—The Bell Telephone Company was officially formed. The company turned into one of the biggest companies in the world, although Bell himself sold most of his shares by 1883 and had very little personally to do with the company after it became successful. The first telephone exchange began operation on January 28, 1878, in New Haven, Connecticut, and as improvements were made to both the telephone itself and the telephone operating system as well, telephones began to show up in homes and businesses all over the country. When Bell's basic patents expired in the early 1890s, almost 5,000 small telephone companies sprang up to go into the business. The telephone soon became the most common tool for personal communication in the United States.

December 6, 1877—Thomas A. Edison recorded the poem "Mary had a little lamb…" on what he called his "talking machine," but which soon became known as the phonograph. As was the case for so many inventions of this time, Edison set out to build an improvement on the telegraph, but ended up with an entirely new device that also borrowed from Bell's telephone concept. Edison intended his machine to be used in dictating applications in business, and was not happy when others saw its potential as a device for mass communication and entertainment. Edison did not want to be involved with a "toy." Nonetheless, a patent for his "phonograph or speaking machine" was granted on February 19, 1878.

May 4, 1886—Patents were awarded to the team of Charles Sumner Tainter, Chichester Bell (a cousin of Alexander Graham Bell), and Thomas Edison, for an improved phonograph. This model included an electric motor, developed earlier by Edison, which drove the recording disk at a constant speed. The recording disks were still cylindrical.

The following year, in 1887, an American citizen born in Berlin named Emil Berliner developed a device using flat disks rather than cylinders. He called his device the "gramophone." In addition, Berliner's system had grooves of constant depth, but varying in lateral direction as the volume of the sound being recorded varied. Edison's basic design used grooves that did not vary in lateral direction, but varied in depth as the volume of the sound changed. His method at the time was known as the "hill and dale" method. Berliner's approach became the standard for the industry, but even though his technique was superior to Edison's, it would take another thirty years before orchestral recordings could be made with reasonable fidelity. In the meantime, many people were satisfied to buy the new "records" to hear celebrities sing and speak.

1888—Heinrich Hertz published a paper titled "Electromagnetic Waves and Their Reflection" describing his experiments since 1886 in which he proved the existence of the electromagnetic waves hypothesized by James Clerk Maxwell in 1873. The Hertz's prime intention was to verify Maxwell's theories, and Hertz never tried to develop a method of communication based on the theory. In fact, when questioned about the possible use of the waves for communication, Hertz said that it probably would never work. However, his work was so important in the development of "wireless communication" that the waves he demonstrated were called "Hertzian waves," and the waves' frequency was measured in terms of "Hertz per second," with one cycle per second being designated one Hertz per second. Hertz brought the idea of wireless communication tantalizingly close, and Guglielmo Marconi made it a reality in just a few more years. In fact, a teen-age Marconi read the results of Hertz's experiments that were published in an electrical journal in 1888 and set out to make experiments of his own. This was the direct connection from Hertz to Marconi.

March 12, 1889— A man named Almon B. Stowger filed a patent for an automatic electromechanical switching device which would connect telephone callers automatically to the number requested without going through the switchboard operator. This device soon spread throughout the telephone systems of the time, and the "Stowger switch" lasted until well into the twentieth century. Stowger was an undertaker who allegedly grew furious at his local switchboard operator because she was connecting all the calls coming through her switchboard for "an undertaker" to her husband, who happened to be an undertaker. Stowger's invention bypassed the switchboard operator, which was one reason it spread so rapidly throughout new telephone systems.

August 24, 1891—Thomas Edison filed a patent for what he called his "Kinetograph" and his "Kinetoscope." Edison had earlier filed a caveat for a patent along similar lines on October 17, 1888. The Kinetograph was essentially the first effective motion picture camera, and the Kinetoscope was the first effective motion picture projector. Edison's major breakthrough was that he printed images on transparent film that could be *projected*. People for years had been running images of sequential pictures in such a way that the viewer was given the sense of motion thanks to the persistence of vision in the eye. But with a projector, people could actually see "moving" pictures on a screen of some sort, i.e. movies. Edison then developed the camera to go with this system, and thus he had the two key elements of a movie system: a camera that would take images in such a way that they could be projected on a screen, and thus form a movie system.

Many people had been working on this system, including a number from Edison's own staff, but it was standard procedure for Edison to file the patent for items developed in his lab. It's possible that others made larger contributions than Edison did to the new "movie" system, but there was no doubt that Edison had a much more marketable name than any of his assistants.

May 9, 1893—The first public demonstration of Edison's new movie system was held on this date in New York. This was essentially a "peep show," because only one person could look into the system at one time. However, in France, developments based on Edison's concepts were going ahead so that it was possible to project a picture on the wall of a theater. Edison had not patented his system outside the United States, but he turned his hand quickly to match the work that was going on in France.

April 23, 1896— By this date, Edison had developed what he called the "Vitascope." With the Vitascope, pictures could be projected in a theater, so that everyone could see the film at the same time. In this sense, April 23, 1896, marked the first movie shown in the United States.

Later the same year, William Dickson, who had previously been associated with Edison at the Menlo Park laboratories, led a group that developed the "Biograph," a device that produced sharper images than the Vitascope. Dickson named his company American Biograph, and it turned out to be the first American motion picture production company.

June 2, 1896 — Guglielmo Marconi of Italy filed a patent in England to cover his work on wireless communication. Marconi was the son of independently wealthy Italian and British parents, and after conducting experiments on his Italian estate and failing to interest the Italian government in the work, he used his mother's British contacts to move to London where there was definite interest in his work. Marconi was only 22 years old when he filed for his patent.

Marconi was working on wireless communication using the dots and dashes of Morse code, and his patent was specifically for a system of "telegraphy" using "Hertzian" waves. Wireless communication using radiotelephony, i.e. human speech, would not be done on a wide scale for another quarter-century. Thus Marconi was not the inventor of radio, as he is often inaccurately called. He was clearly the inventor of wireless communication by what he came to call "radio" waves, and this was his field of interest. But he neither invented nor worked in the field of what we know as "radio."

March 28, 1899 — Marconi sent the first international wireless message from Dover, England, to Wimereux, France, a distance of 31 miles. The British post office and military had been very much interested in licensing his 1896 patent, but, impatient with the pace of progress in the standard government bureaucracy, Marconi formed his own company in 1897 to sell communication products based on his discoveries. One of his first customers was the British military, then involved in the military actions in South Africa that finally produced the Boer War (which officially began in October 1899).

April 26, 1900 — Marconi received a patent for a "tuner" system that allowed simultaneous transmissions on two different frequencies, thus permitting two adjacent stations to operate without interfering with each other. This tuner system was later used by American Marconi, the company Marconi formed in the United States in 1899 to go along with the Marconi Company he had formed in England in 1897.

December 12, 1901 — Marconi completed two days of the first transatlantic wireless communication on this date, transmitting from Poldhu, England, to St. Johns in Newfoundland, a distance of about 2,100 miles. John Fleming, an associate of Marconi and a later inventor of the vacuum tube diode, steadily transmitted the letter "s" at certain time intervals and it was received in Newfoundland on two successive days.

The transmission of just a single letter in Morse code shows once again that all of the transmissions made by Marconi and his contemporaries were "radiotelegraphy." As noted before, Marconi is often called the inventor of radio, but this is incorrect. With certain very isolated exceptions of experiments in "radiotelephony," where the human voice is transmitted rather than Morse code, all of the "wireless communications" for the next two decades were made in the form of Morse code, and they were primarily intended to go from point A to point B. The true development of radio, as we know it, where "radiotelephony" signals were transmitted randomly into the air to be received by whoever had a receiving set, did not take place widely until 1920. This "true" radio used much of the communication equipment developed by Marconi and other inventors, but until 1920 most wireless communication was from point-to-point, and was in the form of Morse code. The prime use was in ship-to-shore, ship-to-ship, and international communications.

Marconi was one of the rare inventors who was also an excellent businessman, and he had an engaging personality as well. The branch of his business called American Marconi that he founded in United States in 1899 had much to do with the expansion of wireless communication in the world, and it was to play a key role in the development of the true radio business in the United States, even though Marconi would not be personally involved.

November 1904— John Ambrose Fleming, an associate of Marconi who took part in the first wireless transmission across the Atlantic in 1901, invented and patented a vacuum tube diode in this month. Fleming in 1904 was following up on the work of Thomas Edison in 1883, where Edison had noted what later was called the "Edison effect": a stream of electrons was given off by a hot filament in a vacuum tube. Fleming used the effect to produce a rectifier that would turn alternating current into direct current. Because of his English background, Fleming called his device a "valve" that conducted current in only one direction, but the name "diode," due to the two active elements in the tube, soon prevailed in the United States. Fleming's invention was basically the first radio tube, and although it was used in a small way as an electronic detector in wireless applications, its primary importance probably was the fact that it led directly to the "audion" tube soon developed by Lee De Forest in 1906 and patented in 1907.

November 25, 1906— On this date inventor Lee De Forest came up with what would prove to be the single most important invention in the development of what we now know as radio. De Forest added a third element (the "grid") to the vacuum tube diode invented by John Fleming in 1904.

De Forest finally named his invention (patented in January 1907) the "audion" tube. In decades of subsequent frantic activity in both the radio and movie businesses, De Forest never made an invention as important as his audion.

However, it is evident, based on subsequent statements, that De Forest did not know how his device worked, nor why it produced great improvement in the circuits in which he employed it. In a later patent application he would state he was "unable to explain this behavior of the audion." It remained for others to discover how the audion worked and to make significant improvements on its use in a way that affected the development of radio to a far greater degree than De Forest was able to do. But no matter what contributions others later made, at the heart of their designs was the tube De Forest invented on this date.

De Forest earned a Ph.D. in electrical engineering from Yale in 1899. He was obsessed with "fame and fortune" and hoped to attain both through great inventions he would make. But he was little more than a dupe when it came to business. He was involved with founding a number of ultimately unsuccessful companies, and his first was typical of the rest. It was little more than a vehicle for fraudulent sales of stock, and its president saw a chance to make a killing in the market by using De Forest's work (some of which had successful moments as De Forest took on Marconi in the field of wireless radiotelegraphy) as a come-on to unwary investors. The head of that company ended up in jail. In a later company, De Forest himself was accused of a similar kind of fraud, but he was finally found innocent by a jury even though the president of that company as well was found guilty.

De Forest was often to suffer such business reversals and make a number of bad business decisions (including trying to steal the patents of others) in his desire to win a fortune. At the time he invented the audion tube, he been working for some time on vacuum tubes and the "Edison effect," but he never gave any credit to either Edison or Fleming for their prior efforts in the field. De Forest ultimately filed over 300 patents, but many were the result of furious work in the laboratory with an eye towards filing possibly lucrative patents whether or not the device actually worked well or he understood fully how it worked.

De Forest shows up often in the story of the development of radio, but he was more an "electronic hustler" than a serious developer of a new art. Still, he has to be credited with the invention of the biggest prize of all, the audion tube.

December 24, 1906— On Christmas Eve, 1906, inventor Reginald Fessenden, who was one of the first American inventors to experiment with radiotelephony rather than radiotelegraphy, broadcast a true "radio" program from Brant Beach on the coast of Massachusetts, south of Boston. Fessenden

played the violin, sang, read from the Bible, and played a phonograph recording. The wireless operators of ships at sea were amazed to hear voices and
music coming through their earphones instead of the dots and dashes of
Morse code. This event essentially marked the start of broadcasting, although
it was in reality only one of the many demonstrations that would be made,
many by Lee De Forest, before radio broadcasting started on a regular basis
in 1920. Fessenden was also "notable" as an inventor from whom Lee De
Forest stole a patented invention in 1903, and Fessenden ultimately was
awarded financial damages in 1906.

January 15, 1907 — On this date Lee De Forest patented his audion tube.
As noted before, the audion, which added a "grid" to the diode and created
a "triode," was the key invention in the beginning of radio. But De Forest
clearly did not understand the workings of the audion, and this would lead
to a long legal battle with inventor Edwin Armstrong, who was the true
"father" of radio from the standpoint of key inventions. This issue is very
complex in legal terms, but the operation of the audion and the key issues
that arose over its use are briefly summarized below.

The grid De Forest introduced into the audion was a zigzag wire that
was negatively charged, as were the electrons produced by the hot filament.
The electrons traveled at high speed from the filament to the positively charged
plate at the other end of the tube, but some were repelled by the negatively
charged grid. As a result, the number of electrons arriving at the plate could
be controlled by the signal on the grid. Thus a relatively small signal on the
grid caused an identical fluctuation in the large signal coming out of the plate,
in essence acting as an amplifier. The larger the amplification, the larger the
"gain" of the tube. De Forest noted the good results of the tube, but he did
not understand why they occurred.

Further, it is now known that with the proper adjustments in the exter-
nal circuitry an amplifier will produce more and more gain and ultimately
turn into an oscillator, in what is called a "feedback" or "regenerative" system. An oscillator serves nicely as the transmitting element in any wireless
system. Thus, in one tube, De Forest had all the elements needed to build
a radiotelephony system, i.e. a system that would transmit and receive voice
messages and not just the dots and dashes of the Morse code.

Edwin Armstrong was the first person to completely understand how
the audion worked, and he designed the first workable regeneration circuit
in 1912, when he was still an undergraduate at Columbia University in New
York. When Armstrong later applied for a patent, De Forest became enraged
to think that someone else would benefit from future applications of the
audion, and he also felt publicly humiliated by the way the somewhat aloof
Armstrong discussed the development in public and indicated strongly that

De Forest did not understand what he had invented. De Forest deliberately set out to steal Armstrong's regeneration patent, and through a comedy of legal errors he finally succeeded. However, the technical world realized the validity of Armstrong's work over that of De Forest regardless of what naïve (in a technical sense) judges finally ruled. In the rest of this chronology we will list the actions of each man with only passing reference to the legal battle, which went on for almost two decades. More detail is available in the "Empire of the Air" listed in the bibliography. It can be added here that Armstrong became a wealthy man on the strength of his inventions, while De Forest eventually went bankrupt in spite of his legal "victory."

January 13, 1910— On this date, Lee De Forest transmitted a radio program from the Metropolitan Opera House in New York. It featured the famous tenor Enrico Caruso, although opinions were divided on the fidelity of the transmission. De Forest had begun his radiotelephony experiments by transmitting from a building in New York soon after patenting his audion tube in 1907. His intended audience was a number of fellow engineers in nearby buildings, but Navy ships in the Brooklyn Navy Yard gave him another appreciative audience. In 1908 De Forest had transmitted phonograph music from the Eiffel Tower in Paris, before making his opera transmission in New York in 1910. De Forest was still trying to make a big impact in the wireless business, but he was having little luck.

April 14, 1912— The so-called "unsinkable" ship *Titanic* hit an iceberg this Sunday evening (New York time) and began to sink, finally going down with a loss of 1,500 passengers and crew early in the morning of the next day. The *Titanic* was on her maiden voyage and carried many notable passengers on its initial voyage from London to New York. It was one of the greatest disasters at sea in history and was the subject of news stories and official inquiries for many months afterward.

David Sarnoff, a Russian immigrant who was beginning a career that would eventually take him to the top of the Radio Corporation of America (RCA) and earn for him the titles of the father of both radio and television, was then working as a radiotelegraphy operator for the American Marconi Company. At his station atop the Wanamaker department store building in New York, Sarnoff heard distress calls crackling through the static beginning at 10:25 P.M. in the evening: *Titanic* had hit an iceberg and was sinking. The most romantic version of the story that was told thereafter was that Sarnoff stayed at his post for the next 72 hours relaying information about the tragedy while the president of the United States ordered every other wireless station shut down so as not to interfere with Sarnoff's reporting. One break took place while Sarnoff was rushed by taxicab to a hotel to receive a "Turkish" rubdown, and then whisked by another cab to another receiving station to help keep track of the names of the survivors as the list trickled in. When the last survivor's name had been recorded, Sarnoff went off to bed and slept the clock around.

Other versions of the story gave Sarnoff much less individual credit, but the facts were that the *Titanic* did sink and the wireless telegraph operator(s) of American Marconi were first to break the news. There were some complaints that American Marconi had deliberately held back on reporting some of the names of the survivors (since many famous people were aboard the ship, and with roughly only one in three of the passengers surviving, interest was high in who survived and who did not) to help keep the story alive, but this criticism soon blew over.

The incident did much to raise the awareness of the general public about wireless communication, and orders soon poured in to American Marconi for both new systems and equipment to upgrade existing systems. Changes were made in the rules of ship travel intended, among other things, to improve communications in the event of distress calls from ships at sea.

Marconi himself, who ironically had reservations on the planned return sailing of the *Titanic* from New York to London, became a more popular icon. American Marconi's stock skyrocketed, and in essence the electronic news business was born. David Sarnoff, who even before the *Titanic* incident was a protégé of Marconi, began his rapid rise in the higher management levels of American Marconi.

September 22, 1912— Edwin Armstrong, while still an undergraduate student in electrical engineering at Columbia University in New York, successfully tested a "regenerative" circuit using the audion tube on this date. Armstrong had begun working on the audion early in 1912 while he was a junior. He continued his study over the summer break between his junior and senior years, and made his breakthrough in September just before he returned to school for his senior year. One point Armstrong noted was a strange "hiss" just as the tube reached maximum amplification. He did not know it then, but this was the result of the tubes breaking into oscillation of continuous waves (cw). These were exactly the kind of waves needed for use as a transmitting element in radiotelephony. Armstrong set out to study this phenomenon as he returned to school.

January 31, 1913— Unable to raise the money for a patent application, Armstrong took the advice of a friend and had a document showing his regenerative circuit notarized by a notary public. Armstrong was very reticent by nature, and word of his new powerful amplification circuit leaked out very slowly. Armstrong was very secretive about his work, keeping practically no records of what he was doing. This would cost him dearly in the future. However, Armstrong was not initially motivated by thoughts of fame and fortune; he just wanted to know how things worked. In this respect, he was the complete opposite of Lee De Forest.

March 12, 1913— As word of Armstrong's receiver continued to grow, one of the members of the faculty at Columbia came out to hear the receiver and discuss its workings with Armstrong. This was the first of other faculty visits, and the professors tried to convince Armstrong to patent the circuit and to pursue its use as a transmitter as well as a receiver. The secretive Armstrong listened very politely, but could not be pushed into action.

June 13, 1913— Armstrong graduated from Columbia and accepted a position as an assistant to the head of the electrical engineering department. Armstrong would receive a good income as an instructor to a Navy class in wireless. In addition, he would have the run of a well-equipped laboratory to continue his experiments. Armstrong was advised by an excellent patent attorney known to the Columbia instructors to file for a patent as soon as possible. But in his normal independent way, Armstrong would not get around to it until four months later.

July 1913— Unaware of Armstrong's work, Lee De Forest sold the rights for his audion tube to AT&T for $50,000. The Bell Telephone system wanted badly to extend its service coast-to-coast and they needed an amplifier (repeater) to do so. De Forest had discovered, more or less by accident, that two audion tubes operated in cascade made an excellent telephone amplifier. He had been negotiating with AT&T since October 1912 to sell his audion patent because he badly needed money. He sold to AT&T the rights to use the audion in telephone applications only.

October 29, 1913— Armstrong finally filed for a patent on his regenerative circuit, but he filed for its use only in receiving applications. Because he did not yet know his lawyer well, Armstrong did not want to disclose the use of his circuitry as an oscillator. This was to prove to be a crucial mistake, but Armstrong would retain for all of his life the feeling that only he knew what was best, and accordingly he would fail to heed much good advice.

November 4, 1913— On this date, Lee De Forest, who also lived in New York, came to Columbia University to give a talk on "The Audion Amplifier" to the Institute of Radio Engineers. After his talk, supposedly De Forest met with Armstrong because word of Armstrong's receiver had by then reached even De Forest. It is not clear if the two men met on this date or on some other occasion near this date. The head of the electrical engineering school at Columbia did not like De Forest because of his questionable ethics and it is certain Armstrong was warned accordingly. Whatever the exact date of their meeting, both men were as far apart as two men could be in terms of personality and ethics. Their meeting did not go well, and it began a lifelong relationship of strong animosity and vindictiveness between De Forest and Armstrong. In the simplest terms, De Forest had "seller's regret" in the sale of his patent to AT&T when he learned what Armstrong had done with "his" audion. De Forest essentially hated Armstrong on sight and De Forest vowed to show he had discovered the regenerative circuit first.

December 8, 1913— Armstrong finally applied for a patent on the use of his regenerative circuit as an oscillator and thus as a transmitter of continuous radio waves. This basically marked the end of the huge rotating devices previously used as transmitters, not to mention spark discharge devices.

December 24, 1913— On this day before Christmas, David Sarnoff led a delegation of three American Marconi engineers to a basement laboratory in Philosophy Hall at Columbia University to meet with the head of the electrical engineering department and his brilliant assistant, Edwin Armstrong. The men from American Marconi were impressed with Armstrong's receiver, and Sarnoff and Armstrong took to each other. They would be friends for decades in spite of some bumps along the way.

Armstrong and Sarnoff met a month later on January 30, 1914, in an American Marconi transmitter "shack" to set up the receiver and listen to Marconi messages from around the world. It was brutally cold, but both men would remember warmly for the rest of their lives the day they spent listening to messages together.

March 1914— De Forest filed a patent for an "ultra-audion" which he claimed would do the work of Armstrong's device without using the regenerative circuit, but his patent application was rejected when the patent examiner found Armstrong's regenerative circuit buried in the maze of paperwork filed with the patent. De Forest decided to go back to the approach of claiming he had discovered regeneration first.

October 6, 1914— A patent for his regenerative circuit was issued to Armstrong on this date. However, Armstrong initially was not able to interest anyone in licensing his patent except the Telefunken Company of Germany. Telefunken had to depend on wireless communication between the United States and Germany after the British cut the undersea telegraph cable to Germany when World War I started in 1914. The arrangement was terminated when the United States entered World War I in 1917. However, in the fall of 1915, American Marconi took out a license on the patent.

March 1915 — Armstrong delivers a technical paper titled "Some Recent Developments in the Audion Receiver" to the Institute of Radio Engineers. It was a detailed report on how the audion could be used as both a sensitive receiver and a generator of oscillator waves, and the paper contained much new information. Unfortunately, it ended with the comment that "I want to point out that none of the methods of producing amplification or oscillation depend on a critical gas action." This was a deliberate slap at De Forest, who at one time in his search for how the audion worked decided that a crucial factor was the gases left in the tube after it was sealed to produce a vacuum. De Forest tried introducing many different gases into the tube without success, and was made to look foolish when it was shown that the purer the vacuum and the fewer extraneous gases left the better.

De Forest was granted a chance to reply, and he chose to attack Armstrong's conclusions, but he added ominously that he had discovered several years earlier that the audion could be made to oscillate. This indicated the direction he was going to take in his patent battle.

April 7, 1915 — Commercial transcontinental telephone service began between the east coast and the west coast of the United States on this date. A few months earlier, in January 1915, Alexander Graham Bell in New York and Thomas A. Watson in San Francisco made a demonstration call, with Bell repeating his famous sentence from 1876 asking Watson to "come here," and Watson jokingly replied that in this case it would take him a week to respond. The mayors of New York and San Francisco later made a demonstration call before commercial service was inaugurated.

The ability of Bell Telephone to start such a transcontinental service was due to the patents they had purchased from Lee De Forest in 1913 for "telephonic" applications. Now that the technology existed to reproduce the human voice over such distances on the telephone, "radio broadcasting" of speech rather than Morse code was not far away.

September 1915 — De Forest now applied for a patent on an "oscillating audion." He acknowledged that a regenerative circuit was needed in the device, but this time he claimed to have discovered the circuit "by chance" in 1912. It was an audacious move by De Forest, but in 19 years, after rulings in 13 different courts, De Forest would win a surprising legal victory in the Supreme Court. The victory would be a legal one only as the technical community disdained the "victory" and considered Armstrong the true inventor.

April 1917— Lee De Forest sold the rest of his audion tube rights to AT&T, collecting $250,000 for his trouble. He had been negotiating the deal since late 1916, and completed it just as the United States was entering World War I. De Forest's latest company, the De Forest Radio Telephone Company, had recently been paying good dividends (a respectable chunk of which went to De Forest himself) as orders poured in from foreign countries already in the war and from the United States military as it got ready for its expected entry into the conflict.

De Forest saw it as the ultimate triumph in his hopes of getting rich from his inventions. Once again, however, he suffered seller's regret, realizing he could have made more from licensing than from selling his patents as more and more communications equipment was sold. He struggled with patent litigation against Armstrong and even with an old suit with American Marconi, and his fortune began to shrink. De Forest had a personal life that was as undisciplined as his professional life (he made and lost three fortunes and was married four times), and in the 1930s De Forest had to declare bankruptcy. In the meantime he would ride high for a while on his patent sales.

April 6, 1917— The United States declared war on Germany and its allies after a series of events following Germany's declaration of unrestricted submarine warfare on January 31, 1917. This resulted in a huge demand for telephone systems to be used in combat, and the U.S. Army Signal Corps installed over 100,000 miles of wire in France to connect 2,600 telephone stations and about 100 switchboards. Armstrong went to Europe as a captain in the Signal Corps.

The Navy took over all commercial wireless activities for the duration, and greatly expanded their capacity for communication, including some radiotelephone services that were used to keep President Woodrow Wilson in touch with Washington when he sailed to the Paris peace conference in December 1918. During the war, the Navy decreed a moratorium on all patent suits related to wireless communication, and they forced the companies involved into a patent-pooling arrangement which would permit the manufacturing of communication equipment to proceed as needed by the war effort. This patent-pooling experience would prove very valuable to the companies involved after the war when efforts were underway to launch the radio broadcasting business.

The war also turned the radio business from a near-"hobby" business into an industrial force. Before the war tubes were made in the hundreds with unsophisticated manufacturing techniques. During the war companies learned to make tubes in the thousands under the watchful eye of government inspectors. The Corning Glass Company supplied cylindrical glass tube blanks in the thousands, and a Belgian-born chemist working in New York named Leo Baekeland built bases for the tubes using a new material called "Bakelite." The tube pins projecting from the Bakelite base fit easily into a standard porcelain and metal socket, thus making the overall assembly of equipment using the tubes much easier. "Radio" would be ready to be born after the war, and the thousands of men receiving training in wireless and the use of wireless equipment would form a core group of listeners to initial broadcasts.

November 11, 1918— World War I officially ended on this date, the first "Armistice Day." The U.S. Navy wanted to take over "radio" as a permanent government monopoly because the Navy clearly saw how crucial communications were to future military success. Congress did not agree to the monopoly status, and did not pass the bill the Navy wanted. However, the government as a whole saw clearly how important communications were to the country. The Navy and Congress were very uncomfortable with the part that American Marconi, essentially a British-controlled company, played in communications. So, during 1919, a concerted effort was undertaken to force American Marconi to sell out to its American competitors.

February 8, 1919— Edwin Armstrong filed for a patent in the United States for his "super heterodyne" receiver. This grew out of his work during the war in an effort to find an unusually sensitive receiver to search for low-level German signals. Armstrong had filed a patent for the receiver in France on December 30, 1918, and partly because of his work on this receiver he was promoted to Major Armstrong early in 1919. He was invited to lecture on radio at the Sorbonne in Paris, received the French chevalier de la légion d'honneur from the head of the French military communications, and was notified that the Institute of Radio Engineers in the United States had awarded him its first medal of honor for his invention of the regenerative circuit. When Armstrong finally returned to the United States in the fall, the Radio Club of America gave a dinner in his honor for his war service and inventions. Major Armstrong had obtained the fame Lee De Forest had lusted after, and Armstrong would soon become wealthy — very wealthy — as well.

October 17, 1919— Late in 1919 a deal was struck for American Marconi to sell out to General Electric (GE), which traced its lineage back to Thomas Edison, and was a major wireless communication/electronics equipment manufacturer. GE then formed a subsidiary called the Radio Corporation of America (RCA), which was incorporated in the state of Delaware on this date. RCA formally took over the operation of American Marconi's assets on November 20, 1919. Westinghouse and American Telephone and Telegraph (AT&T), two other huge players in the communications field, joined

GE as investors in the new corporation. AT&T sold its shares in 1923, but GE and Westinghouse remained prime shareholders in RCA until they were forced to sell in 1932 as part of an antitrust settlement. David Sarnoff, the "hero" of the *Titanic* disaster, came along to RCA as an established executive with American Marconi. The stars were now aligned for the birth of the "radio telephony broadcasting" business, or simply "radio broadcasting" as we know it now.

January 31, 1920— David Sarnoff, then commercial manager of RCA, wrote a 28-page memo to Owen Young (chairman of the board of RCA and eventually of GE as well) outlining Sarnoff's ideas for what he called a "Radio Music Box," an idea Sarnoff said he had proposed to his supervisors at American Marconi in 1916, but which had never progressed very far because of the entry of the United States into World War I.

Sarnoff's idea was that radio's biggest potential was not as an overseas communication tool but rather as a domestic entertainment medium. Radiotelephony could broadcast music, news, lectures, and other entertainment, and people would buy "radio music boxes" to receive this programming. Sarnoff predicted high profits from the manufacture and sale of these boxes, and he said revenue "might" also be possible from the sale of advertisements for interested companies. Sarnoff predicted sales of as many as one million "boxes" in the first three years if management were quick to act.

There was some interest in Sarnoff's idea, but much immediate work had to be done in cleaning up the details of who controlled what in the patent field. Between them, the three basic investors in RCA (GE, AT&T, and Westinghouse) owned or had bought up rights to most of the critical patents, and RCA owned many patents itself that had come along with the absorption of American Marconi. Cross-licensing agreements were established based on the experience the companies had gained from the pooling of patents ordered by the Navy during World War I. Eventually, helped by some stock sweeteners, RCA arranged things so that in the early days of radio, RCA made good profits from patent licensing fees to independent manufacturers of radio sets as well as profits from building radio sets themselves. RCA was truly king of the business. However, the time spent pulling the patent situation together meant that someone else beat RCA in putting the first official radio station on the air.

September 22, 1920— Horne's department store in Pittsburgh ran advertisements on this date offering "Amateur Wireless Sets for $10 and up." The ad was the result of newspaper articles discussing the activities of a Westinghouse engineer named Frank Conrad. Working in an experimental lab at Westinghouse (whose original headquarters were in Pittsburgh), Conrad had established an amateur radio station named 8XK, and he often played music and gave sports results and so forth for the entertainment of other amateur radio operators in the area. There were quite a few amateur operators spread across the United States who had for years listened to wireless radio transmissions meant for ships at sea, and their numbers had increased following World War I because of the training many of them had received in the war.

Such amateur transmissions were not unusual in the United States, but Conrad's work led to an unexpected chain of events. Taking notice of the popularity of Conrad's station, Horne's installed a demonstration receiver in their store, and then offered identical receivers for sale in the hope of creating a new source of revenue. Westinghouse executives took notice of the Horne store advertisement, and before long plans were underway to convert a radiotelegraphy transmitter to a radiotelephony transmitter and go into the radio broadcasting business to try to get the general public to buy radio receivers.

November 2, 1920—Radio station KDKA of Pittsburgh began regular broadcasting on this date. The first program carried information about the Warren Harding-James Cox presidential election taking place on the same date, and the station added musical selections from a phonograph interspersed with selections from a live banjo player. The station was an immediate success. Other stations had gone on the air before KDKA, but KDKA is considered the oldest radio station in the United States that is still in operation. It used radiotelephony so that its wireless broadcasts were in the range of the human voice and music and not in Morse code; it broadcast continuously with a regular schedule intended for the general public; and it was ultimately licensed by the government to provide such a service. By the end of 1920, a total of 30 stations had been licensed. The number approached 600 in the next year, and sales of radio receivers were growing into the hundreds of thousands.

March 25, 1921—On this date RCA set in motion a process that would enable it to overtake Westinghouse's lead in the radio broadcasting business. One reason Westinghouse had jumped out in front was that early in 1920 it had purchased rights to the regenerative and superheterodyne patents of Edwin Armstrong for $335,000 (plus a $200,000 "bonus" if Armstrong prevailed in the De Forest suit). Sarnoff wanted to get into the radio business in a big way, and his chairman, Owen Young, agreed. On this date they signed a deal to give Westinghouse one million shares of stock and a percentage of subsequent radio-related orders to RCA in exchange for the Westinghouse patents. Westinghouse became the single biggest corporate owner of RCA.

RCA, which had struck a similar deal with AT&T earlier, now controlled all the key radio patents of De Forest and Armstrong and some other important inventors (RCA had inherited some key patents from American Marconi when RCA was formed). With the patents it now controlled and its prior cross-licensing agreements, RCA had control over some 2,000 patents and was the "900 pound gorilla" of the radio industry. With this control in hand, David Sarnoff set out to make the radio something everyone would want to own.

July 2, 1921— This was the date of the heavyweight championship fight between champion Jack Dempsey and French challenger Georges Carpentier. It was held at Boyle's Thirty Acres in northern New Jersey just outside New York city, and a record 90,000 people watched as Dempsey won by a knockout in the fourth round. The significance of the fight from a communications standpoint was that about 300,000 people heard it on the radio in a great publicity stunt organized by David Sarnoff.

This single event, more than any other, triggered a great demand for radio receivers. The development of loudspeakers rather than individual earphones and simple dial-tuning systems rather than the use of "cat whiskers" made the radio very easy to use by anyone, turning the radio into a "utility" like water and gas and the telephone. With entertaining programs and news beginning to fill the airwaves, everybody wanted a radio. Sales soared.

March 13, 1922— The first round in the Armstrong vs. De Forest battle went to Armstrong. On this date the court of appeals turned down De Forest's appeal of a May 17, 1921, decision that had gone to Armstrong. The judges in both decisions had issued strongly worded opinions in favor of Armstrong. In normal circumstances this would have been the end of the battle, but the personal hatred between the two men was so strong that it was not. Because De Forest was short of money once more, the normal step would be for Armstrong to waive any costs he was awarded, a final judgment would be issued, and the decision would become final.

Armstrong, however, considered De Forest nothing less than an attempted thief, and he was determined that such an unethical person should be punished for his actions. In many ways Armstrong saw things in clear black and white, and as explained in the Introduction, this would prove to be a big problem for him and those around him. Armstrong's lawyer, as patiently as one could, had told him in essence that things were often shades of gray in the real world and especially in patent infringement cases. Armstrong refused to listen and insisted on payments in the case. In addition, a year later, while the case was still not closed, Armstrong raised a banner on the top of his old homemade aerial at his boyhood home with his patent number clearly printed on it. He knew De Forest could see it from his own home. Stung by Armstrong's actions, De Forest hit on a new approach to continue the case. De Forest knew from considerable experience in patent litigation, as did Armstrong's lawyer, that language rather than the bare facts of the case was the key to winning a ruling. After much time spent reading Armstrong's patent, De Forest hit on the proper combination of words to create a winning case in 1924. March 13, 1922, marked the high point for Armstrong in this case. Afterwards he would simply "snatch defeat from the jaws of victory" because of his unyielding ego and personality.

June 30, 1922— Anxious to lock up the future inventions of Edwin Armstrong for the private use of RCA, David Sarnoff on this date concluded an agreement with Armstrong to pay Armstrong $200,000 plus 60,000 shares of stock for rights to Armstrong's latest discovery of "superregeneration." This discovery, made almost by accident by Armstrong's standards, was to be the next step up from his regeneration circuit. In addition, Armstrong agreed to give RCA the right of first refusal on any of his future inventions.

Armstrong now held the largest number of RCA shares held by an individual shareholder. Armstrong soon proved the value of the deal to RCA by coming up with an improvement to his superheterodyne circuit in 1923 that made RCA's "Radiola" much easier to manufacture on the assembly line and much easier for owners to tune for maximum performance. Armstrong received another 20,000 shares of stock for the rights to this improvement.

August 1, 1923— RCA opened its new radio station, WRC, in Washington, D.C., on this date. RCA had introduced its new radio, the Radiola, the year before to take advantage of the growing sales of radios. The new WRC station was opened to tie in with the boom in the sales of radio sets. During 1922, Herbert Hoover, then the secretary of commerce, had announced "one of the most astonishing things that has come under my observation of American life." He pointed out that the Department of Commerce had estimated that between 600,000 and one million radios had been sold in the last "four or five months" whereas less than 50,000 had existed a year earlier. The interest in radio had become a craze, as more than 200 manufacturers of radios and over 5,000 parts distributors had sprung up.

June 2, 1926— An inventor named C. Francis Jenkins applied for a United States patent on a mechanical television receiver using quartz rods in a rotating drum through which light passed to form an image. This caused a temporary boom in the stock of the company formed by Jenkins, but it eventually collapsed because the resolution of the mechanical system was too poor. The same fate befell a British inventor, John L. Baird, who applied for a British patent for a similar system about a year later. Although some references credit Baird with inventing television for some earlier work he did, all mechanical systems really represent failed attempts to invent a workable television system. Only a private inventor named Philo Farnsworth, and Vladimir Zworkin of RCA, both of whom who worked on electronic — not mechanical — scanning techniques as described later, succeeded in achieving resolutions acceptable for commercial television.

However, although not recognized as such at the time, the work of Jenkins represents one of the first attempts to use a technology that would become known as fiber optics and that would play a major role in communications technology about 50 years later.

November 15, 1926— David Sarnoff took the next logical step and started a broadcasting network, which he called the National Broadcasting Company (NBC). The network made its debut on this date. There were so many stations willing to sign on that NBC was soon divided internally into the NBC Red and NBC Blue networks. Both prospered until the Blue network was sold two decades later to what became the American Broadcasting Company (ABC) to solve antitrust problems.

January 7, 1927— An inventor named Philo Farnsworth filed his first patent for a "television system" on this date. This filing would trigger a long bitter dispute between Farnsworth and RCA, who had their own inventor named Vladimir Zworkin working in the area of television. Farnsworth would win the patent battle in 1935, but the business vision of David Sarnoff would enable RCA to win the television war, just as they had ultimately won the radio war. As was also the case in radio, television would not come to full fruition until about a dozen years following the first key patent filing. RCA would jump into the television business in a big way in 1939, but World War II would delay everything until the later 1940s.

October 6, 1927— The film *The Jazz Singer* debuted in New York City on this date. Featuring Al Jolson, this movie was the first feature-length film that was considered a "talkie," although much more of the film was musical than was dialogue. The movie used the "Vitaphone" sound system developed by Warner Brothers in conjunction with Western Electric (Bell Telephone). The film was not that well received at first, but it was a sensation out in the heartland of the United States, and when it was rebooked into New York in 1928, it grossed $100,000 a week.

The Jazz Singer revolutionized the movie industry and soon all films were "talkies." In a note of irony, Lee De Forest had found the radio business "too crowded" and in 1919 he started work on devices to permit films to "talk."

He invented a system called Phonofilm that made it possible to synchronize a sound track with the picture appearing on the screen. However, by 1928 De Forest had run through his personal fortune trying to develop and promote the company. All he had to show for it was the $100,000 he had received for an option on exclusive use of the phonofilm process, and $60,000 he was later awarded in (characteristically) a patent infringement suit. He had only bitter memories of his involvement, but in 1959 De Forest was given an honorary Oscar for his contribution to what ultimately became the modern motion picture.

September 1928— Bill Paley took over a failing competitor to NBC and turned it into the Columbia Broadcasting System (CBS). From this time onwards until their deaths some decades later, David Sarnoff and Bill Paley, and their respective networks NBC and CBS, would wage a relentless competitive war with each other. The two men would become synonymous in the public's mind with radio broadcasting and the most popular radio programs. They were officially "friendly competitors," but Sarnoff and Paley were as different personally as two men could be, and there was no love lost between them.

October 29, 1928— The Supreme Court upheld the 1924 award of the patent for regeneration to De Forest. As described in the entry for March 13, 1922, Armstrong "shot himself in the foot" by stubbornly refusing to close the case decided in his favor in 1922 and making the decisions in that case inapplicable to the new case brought by De Forest. Ironically, De Forest got nothing from the legal victory except "bragging rights" over his rival. RCA owned the rights to the patents of both Armstrong and De Forest through its prior agreements with Westinghouse and AT&T. In fact, RCA would benefit from the award to De Forest because it effectively added 10 years to the period of time it could collect royalties. Armstrong's patent expired in 1931, 17 years after it was awarded, as all patents do. De Forest's patent dated from the time it was first awarded in 1924, and thus RCA could collect royalties on it until 1941.

December 26, 1933— Edwin Armstrong was awarded a series of five patents for what was to become known as FM (frequency modulation) radio. Armstrong was sure this would become the radio of the future. RCA, which still held the right of first refusal on any new patent obtained by Armstrong, was not so sure. FM radio had better fidelity than standard AM (amplitude modulation) radio, and FM eliminated the static that was such an irritant on AM radio. But RCA, in the person of David Sarnoff, was not so sure people would be willing to pay the higher cost of FM radio to get better fidelity, and RCA itself was pouring the majority of its research funds into television, which Sarnoff was sure people would definitely be willing to pay higher prices to obtain. Sarnoff listened politely as Armstrong pressed for his new system, but RCA made no move to exercise its options on Armstrong's patents.

October 8, 1934— In what was truly the end of a patent war that had taken on the aspects of a long-running soap opera, the Supreme Court ruled again in favor of De Forest. Armstrong had pulled a clever end-run to get the case heard again, but once more, in spite of favorable rulings in lower courts, the Supreme Court ruled against Armstrong in a decision that showed complete misunderstanding of the technical facts of the case. The *New York Times* published an editorial calling for patent reform, and letters poured in from engineers decrying the decision, but the Supreme Court would not be swayed.

As part of the brouhaha surrounding the decision, the Institute of Radio Engineers refused to accept the return from Armstrong of the medal the institute had awarded him in 1918 for the invention of the regenerative circuit. Saying it understood the sense of honor Armstrong felt he was expressing in returning the medal now that the courts had ruled against him, the institute once again stated that it considered Armstrong the inventor of the circuit and that he should retain the medal. Ever after Armstrong would list the regenerative circuit among his accomplishments with a footnote noting that there was a "difference of opinion between the scientific community and the courts" as to who was the true inventor. De Forest for his part would fire off letters of outrage at any official publication giving credit for the invention to Armstrong. Each man went to his deathbed hating the other.

July 1935— Philo Farnsworth was awarded patent priority in the design of his television system over Vladimir Zworkin of RCA. However, the ongoing design difficulties of getting a complete television system into a form where it could be offered commercially to the public continued to dog both Farnsworth and RCA. Many television demonstrations continued to take place, but no complete commercial system was forthcoming.

July 1936— Armstrong was granted a license by the Federal Communications Commission (FCC) to conduct experimental FM transmissions. Frustrated by RCA's apparent lack of interest in his FM system, Armstrong decided to spend his own money to demonstrate a working system. Armstrong was determined to build a new industry which he was sure would be a big success.

April 1937— Near the middle of the month, Edwin Armstrong and his wife ceremoniously chopped down a small tree high on the New Jersey Palisades just across the George Washington Bridge from New York City. This was the official start of a site where Armstrong would build a transmitting tower and a small FM station. It was the start of the FM industry, but the industry would unfold in a much different way than Armstrong anticipated.

April 20, 1939— David Sarnoff took a calculated risk and presented a full line of RCA television sets in conjunction with the opening of the World's Fair of 1939 in New York. The theme of the fair was "Building the World of Tomorrow," and Sarnoff introduced the new line of television sets from RCA with a speech titled "Birth of an Industry" in which he predicted that television, on which he was appearing, would become a major entertainment and information medium. In essence, Sarnoff's appearance marked the first time that television had officially covered a news event.

Sarnoff's calculated risk was that he knew Farnsworth had won patent priority and that RCA would have to work out some sort of agreement after the fact with Farnsworth to avoid a lawsuit. In the meantime, Sarnoff had associated the idea of television with RCA in the public's mind and given RCA a big boost in the television wars to come. Now that over 82 percent of all homes in America owned a radio, television was expected to be the next big game in town.

September 1939— Farnsworth and RCA reached an agreement that RCA would pay a fee of $1 million to Farnsworth as well as a royalty on every television set sold. This payment did not make Farnsworth a true competitor to RCA due to his lack of business acumen. RCA was ready to pursue the television market in earnest, but television was unlike radio in one key aspect. Radio basically broadcast only the human voice and music, and few common standards were needed beyond the broadcast frequency assigned to each station. But television was much more complicated in that television broadcasts were a complex series of signals that had to be turned back into a visual picture by each television receiver. In order to permit different broadcast stations and television receivers to be used interchangeably, certain broadcast standards had to be set, and each "channel" on which broadcast signals were transmitted had to be assigned a specific frequency. Television broadcasts used much higher frequencies than radio, and the frequency spectrum taken up by television signals was much wider than that of radio. The Federal Communications Commission (FCC) would have to establish these standards before commercial television could begin.

June 1940— RCA and Armstrong began negotiations for RCA to take out a license on Armstrong's FM patents. Armstrong had already licensed GE (no longer associated with RCA since being forced to sell its interest in RCA as part of an antitrust settlement in 1932), Zenith, Stromberg Carlson, and others. The initial FM tests had gone well, and the future of FM looked promising. RCA offered $1 million for a non-exclusive license, a very generous offer because it meant Armstrong could take the money and still offer licenses to other companies.

But Armstrong was still smarting from RCA's delay in offering to buy a license, and he made statements showing he was still upset about what he saw as RCA's duplicity in not coming to his aid in his battle with De Forest when RCA would realize a financial gain from the whole process because it controlled the patents of De Forest. Armstrong refused the offer and said RCA would have to accept the same terms he had negotiated with the other companies where they would pay royalties on sales of specific items. Armstrong was sure he would make more money that way, for he saw FM as a potential huge moneymaker. Besides, he was pleased in a vindictive way to twist RCA's tail.

Once again, Armstrong's stubbornness and assurance he was the only person who could be in the right served him badly, as it had in the De Forest case. Armstrong's tendency to be vindictive would also cost him dearly as it had in the De Forest case. RCA refused to deal on such terms, and the licensing offer was withdrawn. FM would turn out to be much less successful in the near term than Armstrong forecast, and he would encounter financial difficulties. Armstrong would file a bitter lawsuit when RCA went ahead with its own FM system. The lawsuit would be settled in Armstrong's favor in the 1950s (actually, in favor of his estate), but it would bring only about the same amount of money as he could have had by agreeing to RCA's offer in 1940.

April 1941—The Federal Communications Commission (FCC) finally reached agreement among its members and potential entrants into the television business. The agreement was very well thought out, and it remains essentially unchanged to this day. Unfortunately, on December 7, 1941, the Japanese bombed Pearl Harbor, and the United States was thrown into World War II. Television broadcasting was suspended, and for that matter all manufacture of commercial electronics was also suspended for the duration of the war. Philo Farnsworth's key patents would expire just after the war ended, and he never became a major player in the television business. However, demonstration television broadcasts continued during the war, and a pent-up demand for consumer products was ready to explode as the war ended.

October 1945—The October issue of the magazine *Wireless World* contained an article written by Arthur C. Clarke, the future famous science fiction writer who was then a junior officer in the British Royal Air Force. In his article, titled "Extra-Terrestrial Relays: Can Rocket Station Give World-Wide Radio Coverage?," Clarke assumed manned stations acting as passive reflectors would be required because he had no way of knowing how quickly electronic equipment would become highly sophisticated, especially after the invention of the transistor at the end of 1947. His key contribution was the definition of the orbit to use.

At a height of 22,300 miles above the equator, traveling at a speed of about 7,000 miles per hour, a satellite would appear motionless in the sky because it would make one revolution around the earth in the same 24 hours it took the earth to rotate. Thus, a satellite in this position could relay signals 24 hours a day, and three satellites properly spaced around the earth would permit continuous communication from any spot on earth to any other spot.

Clarke's idea was considered mostly science fiction at the time, but by 1963 Hughes Aircraft Company would launch satellites into exactly the orbit Clarke proposed. They would be called the Syncom series, and were the first of many communications satellites launched into a "geostationary" orbit, so named because satellites in this orbit do not appear to move against the background of the stars. Clarke was slightly ahead of his time, but his time would arrive much more quickly than anyone thought.

January 10, 1946— The U.S. Army Signal Corps bounced an FM radio signal off the moon from a station on the coast of New Jersey. Aside from being a great publicity stunt, the test proved that the higher-frequency FM waves, as opposed to standard AM waves, would go right through the ionosphere and on into space. At the time the military was planning new applications for FM waves, although they really were using the word interchangeably with "high frequency" waves.

April 16, 1946— The first V-2 rocket was fired on American soil on this date. The origins of the V-2 rocket lay in World War II, when Hitler made a last-ditch effort to bombard England with rockets. A group of German scientists, headed by Wernher von Braun, managed to surrender en masse to American forces, and they ended up in the United States trying to build massive rockets to carry missiles. These rockets eventually became part of the "space race" in the late 1950s when their descendants were used to launch satellites. At the time much environmental information was being gained about the earth from these highflying rockets, and their use was invigorating the earth sciences. Ideas about rockets and missiles were being greatly downplayed, at least officially.

Summer 1946— The first electronic computer built in the United States became fully operational during 1946. This was an ongoing project for the government, originally conceived of as a quick way to calculate accurately the trajectory of artillery shells. It was changed so often in development and purpose that it is hard to say when it actually became operational, because the question constantly remained "operational in what form and for what purpose?" The prime developers were J. Presper Eckert Jr. and John W. Mauchly of the Moore School of Engineering at the University of Pennsylvania.

Their computer had 18,000 vacuum tubes, occupied 1500 square feet of space, consumed 130 kilowatts of power per hour, and weighed about 30 tons. It was a long way from even the computers developed commercially just a few years later, let alone the personal computers of today. The computer at the time, and for decades afterwards, was designed mainly for scientific calculating, business management, and controlling certain industrial processes. It wasn't really until the mid-1970s, when the personal computer made its appearance, that computers became a big part of the world of communication.

March 18, 1947 — The FCC, trying to reassure potential investors in the television business, stated explicitly that the existing television broadcasting standards would not change, and further, that no color television standards would be issued in the near future. Thus, companies who were hesitating to move ahead with the television business in case existing standards changed or color television came along quickly to wipe out plain black-and-white sets were encouraged to move ahead.

The sensitivity of the television camera had been greatly improved, much reducing the level of light needed for good television pictures. In the field, AT&T had begun to greatly expand its coaxial cable installations so that television broadcast signals could be easily sent between major cities. Many cities would otherwise be out of reach of each other, as regular high-frequency television broadcast signals could reach only to the horizon before flying off into space. In the latter part of 1947, the long-predicted rush by consumers into television finally began. Starting in the fall of 1947, one million television sets were sold in two years, with the market 80 percent controlled by RCA. Television was a bigger hit than radio had been a quarter-century earlier.

December 16, 1947 — Three researchers at the Bell Telephone Laboratories invented the transistor on this date. In terms of impact on the world that followed, the transistor was the greatest basic invention in communications through the first half of the twentieth century. It introduced the age of the semiconductor, and this change in the method of manufacturing electronic components would lead to all of the great communications inventions made during the second half of the twentieth century through today. The official announcement of the invention of the transistor was not made until January 1948.

The three scientists who invented the transistor were John Bardeen, Walter Brattain, and William Shockley. They shared the Nobel Prize in Physics in 1956 for their invention, and Bardeen later shared a second Nobel Prize in 1972 for work in superconductivity. Shockley later founded his own company in California to work on semiconductors, and it led to the famous Silicon Valley complex in the second half of the twentieth century.

The transistor was essentially the semiconductor equivalent of the audion triode developed by Lee De Forest in 1906. The transistor could produce all of the electrical functions of the triode, but it could do it much faster in a small, light, sturdy package that consumed almost no electrical power. Further, the transistor turned "on" immediately — there was no filament to warm up. Development of transistors led directly to the integrated circuit in the next ten years, and integrated circuits led directly to the microprocessor about a dozen years after that. The microprocessor led directly to the personal computer and the accompanying flow of communications inventions that continues through today.

July 22, 1948 — Armstrong filed suit against RCA for infringing his patents when selling FM components and systems RCA claimed it had developed on its own. Things had not gone well in the last few years for the FM industry. Starting in 1944, several FCC rulings regarding frequencies to be allocated for FM and the way FM stations would be licensed had worked against the switch to FM. Armstrong and his backers had overlooked the capital investment made in AM broadcasting and the tenacity with which AM broadcasters would try to hold on to their business. Also, the possibilities of television were capturing the attention of broadcasters and the public. Once again, the clarity with which Armstrong could see new inventions waiting to be developed did not extend to the business aspect of broadcasting. In this area his vision was somewhat blurred, but he pushed ahead never doubting the correctness of his forecasts. He had stated in 1940 that in five years FM would completely replace AM, but in the real world it was not happening. The suit against RCA dragged on and on, but Armstrong refused all suggestions, including those of his wife, that he simply settle with RCA. His stubbornness was to have a tragic ending this time.

January 7, 1949 — RCA/NBC ran a program they called the "25th Anniversary of Television." Consumers who had just bought their sets in the prior two years were a little surprised to see the 25th anniversary of anything connected with television, but RCA used the filing of a certain patent by Vladimir Zworkin on December 23, 1923, as their excuse for the program. The patent was not ultimately a key one in the technical development of television, but except perhaps for Philo Farnsworth, no one took exception, and David Sarnoff of RCA used the impetus from this program to have himself later anointed as the "Father of Television" and Zworkin as the "Inventor of Television."

March 26, 1953— The first meeting of the United States National Committee of the International Geophysical Year (IGY) took place on this date. The IGY was planned for the second half of 1957 through the end of 1958. A key question was whether to try to launch a satellite as part of the IGY, and at this meeting the answer was no. However, in the fall of 1953, John Baird of Bell Labs presented a paper to the Princeton, New Jersey, branch of the Institute of Radio Engineers outlining three possible types of communication satellites.

December, 1953— The Federal Communications Commission decided to make the RCA color system the standard for the industry, and color television began its slow rise to the top of the television wars. The RCA system had the advantage that all available television sets, even those designed for black-and-white reception, could receive color broadcasts and show them in standard black-and-white formats. At first consumers were reluctant to pay more "simply" to add color to the programs they watched, especially as only NBC/RCA persisted in broadcasting a wide selection of color programs. By 1972 about one-half of U.S. homes had color sets and color television never looked back. Soon the "standard" television set was a color set.

July 1954— President Eisenhower appointed a panel to identify ways to prevent surprise attacks on the United States. Only a few persons knew at the time that Eisenhower was anxious to find a way to launch a surveillance satellite that would over fly key spots on earth without triggering complaints from other countries, notably the Soviet Union.

October 1954— A Rome meeting of the international scientific community endorsed a plan to include a satellite launch as part of the activities of the International Geophysical Year of 1957-58. Both the United States and the Soviet Union began quietly to plan for such a launch.

January 31, 1954— Edwin Armstrong committed suicide by jumping from the thirteenth story of his apartment building in New York. He was despondent over the progress of his lawsuit with RCA, which even his wife had told him not to pursue. Armstrong and his wife had a falling-out over the suit, when his lawyers finally convinced Armstrong to agree to end it and accept a compromise settlement. Armstrong had a very hard time accepting the idea of a compromise, a character flaw that plagued him literally to the end of his life. Because of the altercation with his wife, Armstrong was living alone at the time of his death, although he left her an apologetic note. He was clearly the key inventor of the radio business, but his unyielding personality brought him much unhappiness in his personal life.

May 5, 1954— After revealing earlier that RCA had set an all-time high in sales the previous year, David Sarnoff announced at the annual corporate meeting on this date that RCA was about to introduce a 19-inch color television set, and that the new field of television had accounted for 54 percent of RCA's business. People were now much more interested in television than radio, and RCA was still number one in the business.

July 29, 1955— President Eisenhower announced that the United States would launch a satellite as part of the International Geophysical Year (IGY). This went along with the "Open Skies" program the president had announced 10 days earlier in Geneva, and the recommendation made by his appointed "surprise attacks" panel in February 1955 for a scientific satellite to be launched to establish the concept of the freedom of space. Four days after the president's announcement of a planned satellite launch, the Soviet Union announced its intention to launch a satellite during the IGY. In September, the Navy was selected to develop the Vanguard rocket to be used as the launch vehicle for the United States' IGY satellite.

September 25, 1956— The first transatlantic cable specifically intended for telephone calls was laid between Newfoundland and Scotland. The dual pair of coaxial cables was called TAT-1 (Trans-Atlantic Telephone) and was able to handle only 36 voice circuits. The conservative telephone companies hesitated to use the "new-fangled" transistor and so they used 51 vacuum tube repeaters (amplifiers) instead on each of the cable pairs. One of the pair of cables carried eastbound voice traffic and the other carried westbound traffic. The limited capacity of circuits often meant a long wait to have a conversation, as the operator would have to call back when a line was available. In 1988, TAT-8, the first fiber-optic cable laid under the Atlantic, carried 40,000 circuits. But TAT-1 was a start, and it lasted until 1979.

September 25, 1956, marked the beginning of the roughly 30-year era of putting coaxial telephone cables under the oceans. Cables went under the Pacific Ocean to Japan and Australia with stops in Hawaii along the way. The first transistor cable came in 1968. Between the United States and Europe, the coaxial cable technology reached a peak with TAT-6 in 1976. There were 4,000 voice channels in TAT-6 compared to a total of 1,200 voice channels in the previous five TATs added together. TAT-6 cost $179 million, more than double the cost of TAT-5. But on a per-circuit basis, TAT-6 cost $45,000, less than half the cost per circuit of the TAT-5 (on a similar basis, the original TAT-1 cost $1 million per two-way channel). The results of TAT-6 were so good that the telephone consortium building the TATs immediately started working on TAT-7, which was a duplicate of TAT-6. The new TAT-7 added another 4,000 circuits in 1983, but when fiber-optic cables began in 1988, they immediately increased the number of circuits per cable by a factor of 10 (a factor of 1,000 compared to the original TAT-1).

November 2, 1956— The *New York Times* carried an article pointing out that the transistor had "created a boom in the manufacture of hearing aids" due to the small size and low battery-power consumption of the transistor: a technology that owed its start to the interest of Alexander Graham Bell in helping the hearing-impaired had come full cycle and was now helping hearing-impaired people to communicate with the world around them.

January 1957— By this date it was expected that the United States would launch four satellites during the International Geophysical Year of 1957-58, and reviews were being held covering the kinds of satellite experiments to be conducted by the four satellites. Two competing meteorological payloads were being considered, and in February a proposal was made for an inflatable reflective sphere to be used in communication experiments.

February 18, 1957— A South-African-born gastroenterologist named Basil Hirschowitz tested a fiber-optic endoscope (a medical device for looking down a patient's throat and into the stomach) on a patient. Hirschowitz developed the device at the University of Michigan. Later in the year his group licensed the technology to American Cystoscope Manufacturers, Inc., for use in urology applications. Although this was not a communications development per se, it helped trigger serious work in the fiber-optics field. The result would be undersea fiber-optic cables capable of carrying 600,000 telephone conversations at once by the end of the century.

October 4, 1957— The Soviet Union launched the first artificial satellite into orbit around the earth. It was deemed to be just a part of the International Geophysical Year (IGY) of 1957-58, but the launch created a sense of panic in the U.S. military because space was seen as the ultimate "high ground." The reaction to the launch was less a sense of what satellites would mean in the field of communication than what they would mean in the upcoming "space race," and what the launch indicated in terms of the ability of the Soviet Union to build rockets that could launch missiles.

Sputnik stayed up for only 21 days, but on November 4, 1957, Sputnik II was launched. The era of satellites was underway, and they would produce another revolution in the field of communications.

December 6, 1957 — The Vanguard rocket exploded on the launch pad as the United States rushed to launch a satellite to respond to Sputnik. Jokes abounded about "Flopnik" and "Kaputnik." In the watering holes of America, people ordered a "Sputnik Cocktail" — one part vodka and two parts sour grapes. But there was much serious criticism about the publicity surrounding the launch attempt. The next attempt was planned much more quietly.

January 31, 1958 — The United States launched its first satellite, Explorer I, into orbit, gaining at least symbolic parity with the Soviet Union. This time the basic launch vehicle was a modified Redstone rocket, courtesy of the Army Ballistic Missile Agency (ABMA) in Huntsville, Alabama. The Redstone rocket was a more powerful version of the V-2, the latest development of Wernher von Braun and friends. The entire multistage assembly was known as the Jupiter-C. This time there was no announcement before the launch, but there were plenty of leaks.

The lift-off time was 10:48 P.M. Florida time. There were some anxious moments afterward waiting to confirm the satellite was in orbit, but the news finally arrived from California that they could hear the signal from the satellite. The satellite then safely completed its first orbit early in the morning of February 1. In the meantime, when the launch was officially announced in Washington, people filled the streets in Huntsville, Alabama, waving placards that said, among other things, "Move over Sputnik." This launch marked the beginning of a huge investment in satellites of all types, mostly communication satellites, but Explorer I and the satellites that immediately followed were research satellites.

February 1, 1958 — The Advanced Research Projects Agency (ARPA) officially went into business. The stated mission of ARPA was to keep the United States ahead of its military rivals by pursuing research projects that promised significant advances in fields related to the national defense. ARPA did not actually do any work on its own, but initiated projects and then carefully managed the academic and industrial contractors who did the work. ARPA evolved into a prime supporter of computer work being done by universities, and by 1970 its attempt to tie together several large time-sharing computers at several of these universities led to what was called the ARPANET. No one knew it at the time, but the ARPANET was the beginning of the Internet. Thus, the Internet is just one of many descendants of the efforts made to respond to the Sputnik launches by the Soviet Union in 1957.

March 17, 1958—The United States continued its launch program by putting "Vanguard I" into orbit. This was the satellite that collected the data proving the earth was pear shaped.

September 12, 1958—Jack Kilby of Texas Instruments built a working model of an "integrated circuit." This circuit attempted to get around the limitations of reducing transistorized circuits in size which are imposed by the need to connect the transistor to other electronic components to make a functioning circuit. Kilby's model essentially eliminated the need for the other components by building them on the same silicon "chip" as the transistor. This process would not only make the circuit much smaller, it would in the long run make it much cheaper to produce and much more reliable. Texas Instruments filed a patent for the circuit on February 6, 1959, and announced it one month later. Robert Noyce of Fairchild Semiconductor was working on a similar device in January 1959 as described in the entry for that date. Noyce would ultimately win the patent battle.

October 1, 1958—The National Aeronautical and Space Administration (NASA) was created. Its mission was to research the possibilities and challenges of flight both inside and outside the atmosphere. It was a government agency, but not connected to the military, which was pursuing satellites and space programs on its own. NASA's initial focus was intended to be developing passive communications satellites (reflective satellites as opposed to active satellites which carried communications equipment of their own) in low-earth orbits. This charter would soon be modified following new developments in the private sector.

January 1959—Robert Noyce of Fairchild Semiconductor was working on a way to put an entire electronic circuit built around a transistor on a single silicon "chip" to reduce its size and cost and increase its reliability, as described in the September 12, 1958, entry discussing the work of Jack Kilby of Texas Instruments. Noyce concentrated on ways to interconnect the various electronic components while Kilby had concentrated on how to make the components themselves. With a well-thought-out patent application, Noyce and Fairchild were awarded a patent for an "integrated circuit" on April 25, 1961, while the patent application of Kilby and Texas Instruments was still being analyzed. Noyce had won the legal victory, but today both men are considered to have independently come up with the basic idea of integrated circuits.

The integrated circuit was a major breakthrough in the field of manufacturing electronic circuits used in communication devices of all types. It greatly reduced costs and provided much more reliable and more complex circuits. This breakthrough would lead to the microprocessor in another decade, and the microprocessor would lead to the next quantum leap in electronic products, including the personal computer.

October 25, 1959— Two key engineers at the Hughes Aircraft Company in Los Angeles, Hal Rosen and Don Williams, proposed a lightweight so-called 24-hour satellite (now called a geostationary satellite). There were plans unfolding in the military for a 24-hour satellite, but it would be much bigger (and heavier and thus harder to launch) than the one proposed by Hughes. Hughes management was reluctant to commit funds to their engineers' novel idea. No one could know at the time that the satellite proposed by Rosen and Williams would eventually reign supreme in the communications satellite field.

February 1960— Engineers Hal Rosen, Don Williams, and Tom Hudspeth join together at Hughes Aircraft Company and offer personal checks of $10,000 each to continue funding on their 24-hour satellite idea. Management is impressed with their conviction but hesitant to commit company funds. The engineers begin to seek alternate sources of funding, but on March 1 top Hughes management decides to take the risk to proceed with the satellite.

May 13, 1960— NASA's first attempt to launch Echo I failed. Echo was intended to be the first passive communications satellite, although it was essentially only a huge balloon (about 100 feet across) that would be used as a reflector satellite. The balloon was to be inflated once it was in orbit. It was made of polyester and coated with aluminum, not unlike the Mylar balloons now popular at birthday parties.

The Navy had been experimenting with bouncing signals off the moon since 1954, and with a system called Communication by Moon Relay (CMR) the Navy had been regularly communicating between Washington, D.C., and Hawaii since 1959 (the program would continue until 1963).

In the meantime discussions were going on to permit NASA to pursue active satellites with communications equipment on board as well as passive satellites. Bell Laboratories wanted to focus on a fleet of medium-altitude communications satellites (with orbits in the range of hundreds of miles), while Hughes was trying unsuccessfully to develop interest in its 24-hour active satellite.

May 16, 1960— Theodore Maiman demonstrated the first laser at the research laboratories of the Hughes Aircraft Company in Malibu, California. The word "laser" is an acronym for "light amplification by stimulated emission of radiation." Its key advantage is that it generates light waves that are in phase with each other. This light is known as "coherent" light and it means that the output of the laser is at a single frequency, rather than a mix of frequencies such as light from the sun, which consists of light at many frequencies (colors). This permits the output from a laser to be focused, resulting in lasers with high power outputs (the "death-rays" of science fiction), or medium-power outputs for industrial cutting or surgical applications. In communications, the laser can be used as a transmitter that operates at very high frequencies, and thus can carry a great deal more information than radio or microwave broadcasts, which operate at frequencies billions of times lower than light. The development of the laser gave a big boost to the consideration of fiber-optic communication systems, and now that a transmitter was available, improvements were pursued in fiber-optic glass to make complete communication systems a reality.

The laser derived from work originally done by physicist Charles Townes when he developed the "maser" which was an acronym for "microwave amplification by stimulated emission of radiation." The maser became a very sensitive receiver in early satellite communications programs and in certain applications in astronomy, but Townes himself suggested ways to build a laser based on his developments. Maiman of Hughes was the first to actually build the laser. However, that first laser fired only bursts of ruby light, not a continuous wave of light. It was a start, but not yet suitable for communications applications.

August 12, 1960— NASA successfully launched Echo II, the passive balloon-like reflecting satellite it had failed to get into orbit in May 1960. The performance of Echo II was excellent, and it confirmed that even a passive satellite was easier to use than a complicated chain of ground relay stations. The medium-altitude reflector had the expected problem that no antenna on earth could "see" the reflector for any meaningful period of time. Echo orbited the earth once every 90 minutes, and a given station on earth could "see" the satellite for only about ten of those minutes. This was why Bell Labs was proposing a fleet of active satellites at medium altitudes so at least that one satellite would always be in view of a pair of ground stations. The 24-hour satellite proposed by Hughes would by definition be in view 24 hours a day, but it would need to be placed into orbit at an altitude of 22,300 miles.

August 1960— NASA was given the charter to enter the active communications field as well as the passive communications field, although there was an understanding that the Department of Defense would deal with 24-hour satellites and NASA would restrict itself to medium-altitude satellites (up to about 500 miles). However, there was an underlying current of suspicion in the industry about the military's capabilities. The Army had launched an active communications satellite about two years earlier called SCORE; it lasted only 13 days in orbit before failing. Now the Signal Corps was trying again with an active satellite called Courier, and it would last only 17 days in orbit. By the middle of 1961, NASA would be given the charter to pursue 24-hour satellites as well.

September 26, 1960 — The first televised debate between two presidential candidates took place on this date between Richard Nixon and John F. Kennedy. There were three additional debates, on October 7, 13, and 21, but none had the impact of the first. Most experts felt that Kennedy clearly won the first debate by a large margin in terms of appearance and style, and he quickly vaulted from underdog to leader. Over 90 percent of American homes had television sets by this time, so more people saw this debate than had ever seen a single event in any previous presidential election campaign. The debates were credited by analysts as being the most significant single factor in Kennedy's narrow win in November. The debate on this date firmly established network television as the prime instrument of political discourse.

December 12, 1960 — An Iranian-born physicist named Ali Javan, who had studied under Charles Townes, developer of the maser, on this date successfully produced the first continuous-wave gas laser. Javan used helium–neon gases, and his laser became the standard laboratory tool for further studies into lasers. Javan worked at Bell Laboratories; his laser work triggered additional experiments in transmission by light waves in optical fibers, but it would take the arrival of semiconductor lasers in the 1970s to get optical systems into wide use.

May 18, 1961 — NASA announced that RCA won the competition to build a medium-altitude active communications satellite to be called Project Relay. NASA had put out a request for proposal (RFP) for the satellite system in January 1961. Both Bell Labs and Hughes officially submitted bids, but both companies were completely tied up in their own internal satellite programs and they had no passion for Relay. On this same date NASA told Bell Labs that NASA would agree to launch, for a fee, the Bell Labs satellite now generally known as Telstar. NASA was moving into a key position in terms of running communications satellite programs.

May 25, 1961 — President Kennedy made his "moon speech," in which he announced that it was the intention of the United States to send men to the moon and retrieve them before the decade was out. Part of the speech focused on communication (and meteorological) satellites. The speech came just 20 days after Commander Alan B. Shepard Jr. successfully completed the first sub-orbital space flight for the United States. The result of the speech was a great investment in all the equipment necessary to accomplish such a feat, and research and development in communications equipment got a huge boost. The goal was realized in July 1969, just within the end-of-the decade time frame originally proposed.

June 30, 1961— Lee De Forest died about two months short of his 88th birthday. In 1948, he had written an autobiography titled *Father of Radio*, claiming for himself the key role in the development of radio. A prior biography of him had not sold well, and when De Forest's book was published in 1950, it too disappeared with scarcely a trace. Time had passed him by and he remained the "father of radio" only in his own mind.

August 11, 1961— NASA announced that it had given Hughes Aircraft Company a sole-source contract to build a 24-hour satellite to be known as Syncom. NASA had now emerged as the key player in the communications satellite business. As noted in the entry for May 18, 1961, NASA was also conducting Project Relay with RCA and planning to launch the first two of the Telstar satellites being built by Bell Labs.

The NASA action was a result of military concerns that it would not be able to develop a rocket suitable for launching the Army's heavy (and growing heavier) "three axis" 24-hour satellite called "Advent." NASA was thus given responsibility by the military for both the medium-altitude satellite programs (Relay and Telstar) and the 24-hour satellite program. It was decided to try the 24-hour satellite proposed by Hughes, which would be stabilized by spinning like a top instead of by the three-axis technique and thus would weigh only about one-tenth as much as the Army's proposed Advent satellite. Thus, among other things, the Hughes satellite would be much easier to launch.

It was sweet revenge for Hughes. Hughes had received much criticism from the military and even from their competitors for their "unrealistic" proposals over the preceding two years. No one could know it at the time (except perhaps the three Hughes engineers who offered to put up their own funds to support the project in February 1960), but when Syncom was launched in mid–1963, it immediately made obsolete Bell Lab's Telstar and RCA's Relay which had been launched before Syncom.

February 1962— President Kennedy sent the Communications Satellite bill to Congress. It proposed a private company, under close regulation, to run the country's communications satellite business. The company would have 50 percent of its stock owned by the public and 50 percent owned by common carriers in the communications business. The bill was specifically aimed at making sure AT&T, which had a monopoly in the land communications business through Bell Telephone, would not be able to develop a monopoly in space communications as well. Another intent of the bill was to keep private companies like Hughes, RCA, and even Bell Labs, although a part of AT&T, involved in developing space products, which they surely would do more quickly and efficiently than the federal government. Hearings began in Congress to reach the compromises necessary to achieve the purpose of the bill.

July 10, 1962 — Telstar I, the satellite built by Bell Laboratories, was launched. It was an immediate success and created a sensation around the world. In part, the Telstar system was a joint venture between the United States, England, and France. Bell Laboratories built the satellite with its own resources in the United States, but in all three countries large (and expensive) ground stations were needed to "talk" to the satellite. So the telephone companies of all three countries built such ground stations at their own expense. The one used by Bell Laboratories was in Andover, Maine.

Telstar was about three feet in circumference (about one foot in diameter) and it weighed about 171 pounds. The Thor-Delta rocket that was to place it in orbit 500 miles up had a maximum capacity of 180 pounds. Once the satellite had been placed in orbit, all the necessary control systems were checked out. On its sixth orbit, late in the afternoon in the United States, Telstar was switched on and a picture of the ground station in Andover, Maine, was shown simultaneously to television viewers in the United States and Europe. It was the first time live television was seen over such a wide area.

For a number of reasons, primarily the effects on electronic components of unexpected radiation from a nuclear test, Telstar remained fully operational for only four months, and ceased operations in about seven months. Bell Laboratories planned for an eventual fleet of about 50 satellites to be sure at least one of the medium-altitude satellites would always be in view of ground stations here and in Europe. They were building a total of six in the first batch, and Telstar II was planned for launch in 1963. It would be launched as planned, but after the success of the Syncom satellite built by Hughes and also launched in 1963, the Telstar program would be set aside.

August 1962 — J. C. R. Licklider and Weldon Clarke publish a paper titled "On-line Man-Computer Communication." This paper is now considered the first paper on the Internet concept. Licklider was the first director of the

Advanced Projects Research Agency (ARPA)'s Information Processing Techniques Office (IPTO), and as such he was involved in the 1960 paper about "Man-Computer Symbiosis" that was the first to discuss the packet-switching concept that underlies the Internet. The RAND Corporation's Paul Baran had written a paper earlier in 1962 titled "On Distributed Communications Networks" describing his studies on packet-switching networks. (RAND was a private "think-tank" corporation that often worked on government projects.)

What was really new in Licklider's efforts was the concept that computer science and technology should concentrate on serving the needs and aspirations of the human user rather than forcing users to adapt to the machine. Licklider went on to fund programs aimed at interactive computers and time-sharing arrangements. It would be decades before the Internet progressed to anything resembling what we know today, but this period in 1962 was where it started. Computers were still thought of as primarily computing machines, but people such as Licklider were already thinking that they could be used as communication devices as well.

August 31, 1962— President Kennedy signed the bill authorizing the creation of the Comsat Corporation. He had initiated the bill in February and it had finally emerged from Congress this month. Comsat was short for "Communications Satellite Corporation." It was a government corporation that would operate through private companies who would design and build satellites and satellite systems using Comsat funding. These products would then belong to Comsat, the only company in the United States permitted to own and operate communications satellites. Comsat would then sell these services to private communications companies, who in turn would sell them to the public. This would create, it was hoped, the proper mix of private involvement and government control and regulation.

Comsat would work extremely well for the next 40 years, until communications satellites had become so common that they were almost a utility. Then, in 1999, a private company, Lockheed Martin, would take over Comsat and Congress would unravel the Communications Satellite Act so that the takeover could proceed. For most of its lifetime, Comsat would be the representative of the United States to Intelsat, the international consortium of countries that would contract for individual satellites and provide rented satellite services to its member countries. During the startup of Intelsat, Comsat also provided management services to Intelsat.

December 13, 1962— Continuing NASA's feverish efforts to get the communications satellite business off the ground, the Relay satellite built by RCA was launched on this date, but Relay was so much like Telstar that it attracted very little attention.

February 14, 1963— The first 24-hour satellite built by Hughes, called Syncom I, was launched on this date, but communication with the satellite was lost when technicians tried to "insert" the satellite into orbit.

A 24-hour or geostationary satellite has to be placed in a proper orbit 22,300 miles above the earth. To reach that orbit, rockets fired in sequence carry the satellite more or less straight up, resulting in an orbit that is highly elliptical. Its apogee or high point is 22,300 miles high, but its perigee or low point is much lower. A satellite left in this orbit would essentially be useless. A final rocket gives the satellite a "kick in the apogee," firing just at apogee to "circularize" its orbit at 22,300 miles. This also provides the proper speed to keep the satellite in sync with the rotation of the earth so it appears to stay in one spot above the earth. It was during this process that communication with the satellite was lost. Jubilation turned to despair, especially at Hughes. However, there were two more satellites in process behind Syncom I.

May 7, 1963— Telstar II, the second of the Telstars NASA had agreed to launch, was successfully launched on this date. As had been the case with the Relay launch in December 1962, there was a "been there, done that" quality about Telstar II. No one suspected at the time that Bell Laboratories' remaining Telstars would never be launched and the Telstar program would fade away once Hughes launched its next Syncom.

July 26, 1963— Syncom II was launched more-or-less successfully: while this time the satellite reached the 22,300-mile level, it was not exactly co-planar with the equator as a geostationary satellite should be. The final orbit was called a "quasi-geostationary" orbit.

However, there was nothing "more-or-less" or "quasi-" about the success of the satellite. The results were better than anticipated and proved quite clearly that for the purpose of communications as they were defined at the time, geostationary satellites were superior to medium-altitude satellites. Syncom III was launched the next year just in time to permit two-thirds of the world to see live action at the 1964 Tokyo Olympics via Syncom II and Syncom III. When the first Intelsat-sponsored satellite was launched in 1965, it was the newest relative of Syncom called "Early Bird" or Intelsat I. The space consortium would continue to purchase geostationary satellites thereafter. After much struggle, Hughes proved the new era of communications satellites would come in the form of geostationary satellites.

March 1964— Paul Baran, who was working at RAND Corporation on ARPA-related projects (as noted in the entry for August 1962) wrote a paper titled "On Distributed Communications Networks" which could be a blue-print for a nationwide distributed packet-switching network. Baran had been working on projects for the government to find switching systems that would have enough redundancies to provide a communications capability in the event of nuclear attack and the loss of certain switching nodes. An unexpected consequence of this work was a rumor that sprang up to the effect that the Internet had been designed to survive a nuclear war.

Also in 1964, Len Kleinrock wrote a book titled *Communication Nets*, outlining a network design and queuing theory needed to build packet-switching networks. The elements were now at hand to put together what would become the ARPANET, the direct precursor to the Internet as we know it now.

July 1964— Representatives of 18 countries formed a worldwide satellite network now called the International Telecommunications Satellite Organization or Intelsat. It planned to launch satellites and provide satellite services to its members, so that a country could, for example, simply rent some channels on a satellite rather than going to the expense of building a complete satellite system and launching a satellite. The consortium would agree to allocate "slots" in space for satellites so that two countries would not try to put a satellite in the same slot, or put up satellites that would interfere with each other, or permit the messages of one country to be heard by another if privacy were wished.

Each country would appoint representatives to convey its needs and wishes to Intelsat (Comsat would be the representative from the United States), and each country would make payments and/or collect fees as directed by Intelsat. The first commercial communications satellite, called "Early Bird" (later Intelsat 1), would be built by Comsat. The satellite would transmit to earth stations in the United States, England, France, and Germany. This would be the start of satellite services for a fee.

Intelsat has been very successful, and today it has over 100 members offering satellite services to over 200 countries and territories. In 2000, Intelsat generated over $1.1 billion in revenue, nearly exactly as prophesized by John Baird of Bell Laboratories and Telstar nearly 40 years earlier. In 2001 Intelsat became a private company wholly owned by its stockholders. It has continued to expand the services it offers.

February 1965— Larry Roberts, a computer scientist at the Lincoln Laboratories of the Massachusetts Institute of Technology (MIT), who would join ARPA in 1966 and ultimately manage the ARPANET program, received the first ARPA contract for a network experiment.

April 6, 1965— The first Intelsat satellite, initially known as "Early Bird," was successfully launched. It was the first commercial communications satellite, in that it offered satellite services for a fee as arranged by Intelsat. Comsat supplied the satellite under contract to Intelsat, and Comsat chose Hughes as the builder of the satellite and NASA as the provider of launch services. Hughes upgraded its Syncom series to the current state of the art, and on this date a Delta rocket put the satellite into geostationary orbit 22,300 miles above the earth.

Although the satellite represented the best in the technology of the time, it was primitive compared even to what would come soon after. Intelsat 1 did not have a battery suitable for full energy storage and could operate only when it could "see" the sun. It could transmit to only one point at a time, meaning the four countries who had built earth stations to talk to the satellite (United States, England, France, and Germany) could not receive the same messages simultaneously. Even with these defects it was a commercial success. Further, although intended to operate for only 18 months, it performed nonstop for almost four years. Intelsat soon established a global communications system with satellites covering the three major ocean areas.

April 19, 1965— A paper was published in *Electronics* magazine on this date titled "Cramming More Components onto Integrated Circuits." The author was Gordon Moore of Fairchild Semiconductor, the company that was founded in 1957 when Bob Noyce, later to win the patent for the integrated circuit (*see entry for* January 1959), and others left Shockley Semiconductor en masse in a dispute with Shockley. Gordon Moore was head of research and development at Fairchild Semiconductor, and in 1968 would form Intel Corporation with Noyce.

Moore's article showed that the complexity of integrated circuits in terms of how many equivalent transistors could be put on a single "chip" had been doubling every year, and he forecast that the trend would continue. The press dubbed his forecast "Moore's Law" and the name stuck. The law continues to operate today, as the number of transistors per chip has grown from the hundreds to the thousands and into the millions. The "law" has been slightly modified into a doubling roughly every 18 months rather than one year, but research continues to make it operate well past the point when "common sense" says it must ultimately come to an end. It is Moore's Law that produces the apparent dichotomy of ever-increasing complexity in electronic products with ever-increasing reliability, decreasing size, and decreasing costs.

In his paper Moore stated that the increasing complexity might make computers "more generally available throughout all of society," but even he could not see the explosion of personal computers that would come in the 1970s using microprocessors from Intel, his yet-to-be-born company. We have discussed and will continue to discuss the impact of Moore's Law elsewhere in this book, but this date marked its official birth into the world of communications and beyond.

October 1965— For the first time, two computers talked to each other. The demonstration took place at MIT's Lincoln Laboratories under Larry Roberts, who was conducting network experiments as noted in the entry for February 1965.

January 27, 1966— Engineer Charles Kao gave a talk at the London headquarters of the Institution of Electrical Engineers on the subject of fiberoptic communications. The talk was in advance of a paper that would appear in the July 1966 issue of the *Proceedings of the Institution of Electrical Engineers*. Kao took the position that the electrical loss in good optical glass could be reduced below 20 decibels per kilometer, and this level of loss would make glass fibers suitable for use in communications systems.

Many in the communications world grasped the significance of Kao's proposal. Transmitting at frequencies near the frequency of light would greatly increase the bandwidth of the information that could be transmitted. It was noted that experiments with optical wave-guides indicated that 200 television channels or over 200,000 telephone channels could be carried in preliminary optical systems. There remained much work to do, but the paper by Kao started many serious efforts around the world to bring optical communications systems to fruition.

December 1966— The design of the ARPANET began. The program described to Congress would explore computer resource-sharing and packet-switched communication. Just two months earlier the first paper on network sharing, titled "Toward a Cooperative Network of Time-Shared Computers," had been published; it described network experiments to date. The first stages of what would become the Internet were about to be conceptualized.

April 1968— J. C. R. Licklider and Bob Taylor published "The Computer as a Communications Device." This was official notice that with proper design of computers and networks the computer could become a key part of worldwide communications, but still no one could foresee how big a role the computer would play in communications in the future.

July 16, 1968— Bob Noyce, the inventor of the integrated circuit (*see entry for* January 1959), and Gordon Moore, a key co-executive with Noyce at Fairchild Semiconductor and proclaimer of "Moore's Law," signed incorporation papers to start a company called Intel. Fairchild Semiconductor was the firm started by Noyce and others in 1957 when they departed en masse from Shockley Semiconductor, the company founded in 1955 by William Shockley, a co-inventor of the transistor. Many of the key firms that started what became known as the "Silicon Valley" (roughly between San Jose, California, and Stanford University in Palo Alto, California), can trace their lineage back to Fairchild Semiconductor and/or Shockley Semiconductor.

Fairchild Semiconductor had been extremely successful, perhaps in a sense too successful. The East Coast executives of Fairchild exercised their option to buy out Fairchild Semiconductor in 1959. However, the key members of Fairchild Semiconductor, now rich men, began leaving in the 1960s to start their own companies when the controlling hands from the East Coast became too confining. Noyce and Moore were among the last to go. While at Fairchild Semiconductor, Moore, head of research, wrote a famous paper in 1965 (*see entry for* April 19, 1965), observing that with the new integrated circuit, the number of effective transistors per chip was doubling every year and would continue to do so. The newspapers dubbed it "Moore's Law" and the name stuck. Although revised slightly to a doubling every 18 months or so, Moore's Law still holds true. The number of transistors per chip has grown from 1,000 to about 50 million, and is said to be heading towards one billion. With this kind of research progress, Intel would invent the "computer on a chip," the microprocessor, and would become both the biggest and the most important semiconductor company in the world.

December 1968— A contract was awarded to Bolt, Beranek, and Newman (BBN) to begin work on the ARPANET. BBN was a relatively small company located in Cambridge, Massachusetts and had close ties to MIT and Harvard. BBN also had experience in time-sharing and networking. The ARPANET was physically underway.

January 1969— AT&T established the first cellular telephone system on the "Metroliner" train running between New York City and Washington, D.C. The system, employing pay phones on the train, not only used "hand-offs" as the train moved from the range of one tower to the range of another, it also featured "frequency reuse" which is technically the defining factor of a cellular system. Delighted passengers made telephone calls while traveling at over 100 miles per hour on the train. The system was controlled by a computer in Philadelphia.

July 20, 1969— The United States landed men on the moon as nearly the entire world watched on television. Not only did this mark the end of the "space race" in the sense that the Soviet Union was unable to make a response of any kind to this feat, the event marked the ultimate communication accomplishment of the time, transmitting events directly from the moon in real time and displaying them simultaneously around the earth.

September 1, 1969 — The first node of the ARPANET was installed at the UCLA network measurement center in California. Additional nodes were installed on a monthly basis thereafter at Stanford Research Institute (SRI), the University of California in Santa Barbara, and the University of Utah. Once these initial four nodes were functioning smoothly, plans would be implemented to expand the network to 15 computer science sites funded by ARPA across the United States. These nodes were expected to be completed in 1971.

October 1969 — A Japanese company named Busicom gave Intel the go-ahead to build a special chip for the business calculator the Japanese firm wanted to build. Early in 1969, Busicom had commissioned Intel to supply chips for Busicom's line of calculators. The key Intel engineer, Marcian "Ted" Hoff, Intel's employee number 12, had offered Busicom a more powerful chip than was required, one that would contain the equivalent of over 2,000 transistors compared to roughly 1,000 in the best chips available elsewhere. Busicom agreed, on the basis that they would get an exclusive contract for the chip, and the project went ahead.

The "special chip" was eventually named the 4004. It was the first microprocessor, the first "computer on a chip." It was primitive compared to microprocessors of today, but the 4004 was the beginning of a true revolution in the integrated circuit and computer industries.

June 1, 1970 — At 10:30 A.M., according to a note scribbled rapidly by Izuo Hayashi at Bell Laboratories in New Jersey, the first semiconductor laser to operate at room temperature in the United States produced a continuous wave of infrared energy. The note was written for Mort Panish, Hayashi's collaborator, who had been delivering volumes of wafers with various layers of gallium-arsenide material for Hayashi to test.

There had been a vigorous race going on around the world for such a laser because this was a key step in achieving fiber-optic communications. Intensive research was also going on to find ultra-clear (low loss) glass, but without the laser as the key transmitter source, the system would still be incomplete. Unknown to anyone at the time, some Russian scientists had actually edged out Bell Laboratories in the race, creating such a laser a few weeks earlier, on May 5 in Leningrad. There were a number of jokes about the penchant for the Russians to claim to have invented nearly everything, but this claim seemed valid. Unfortunately, nothing came of it as the inventors later disappeared into the Russian bureaucracy. However, several other countries soon made legitimate claims of positive results, and now that the concept had been established, researchers settled down everywhere to improve the reliability of the semiconductor laser.

September 30, 1970— Robert Maurer of the Corning Glass Company in upstate New York presented a paper at a telecommunications conference in London describing—somewhat coyly—the results Mauer, Donald Keck, and Peter Schultz of Corning had achieved over the summer in obtaining ultra-clear low-loss glass fibers. They had obtained 16 decibels loss per kilometer, which was below the "magic" loss of 20 decibels per kilometer that was regarded as the maximum loss level that could be tolerated to make fiber optics suitable for communication purposes. Corning wanted to announce their results, which were truly a breakthrough in the state of the art, but Corning was also very conscious of its historical role in the glass industry where secrets were held very close to one's chest. Even the conference was intended to focus not on fiber optics but on millimeter wave-guides, which were thought to be the next big breakthrough in high-frequency (and therefore high bandwidth capability) communications. Fiber optics were almost a sideshow at the conference.

Thus, the Corning Glass paper did not make a big stir at the conference except among those who happened to be closely involved in research on glass fibers. Among this group was Bell Laboratories who were probably Corning's biggest potential customer for fiber-optic glass. The two companies began a cautious dance, as Bell was deeply involved in glass-fiber research of its own. There were no explosive results from the paper, but in the previous few months Corning had made the major breakthrough that would ultimately lead to the explosion of fiber-optic communications around the world.

October 1970— Intel announced the introduction of a chip it named the 1103. This chip was the first large seller of a class called DRAMs (dynamic random-access memory). DRAMs were semiconductors that could be used for memory storage that had previously been the province of magnetic-core memories in computers. It was a revolution in the computer industry. DRAMs were smaller, faster, and cheaper than magnetic cores. All computer makers eventually switched to DRAMs, and as is usually the case with semiconductors, performance increased as costs fell and semiconductor memories began to be used in many places that magnetic cores had not been. The 1103 chip created a multi-billion-dollar market, and although Intel would withdraw from the market in about 15 years when the Japanese drove prices down dramatically, memory chips were Intel's first big seller, as the founders had planned. Their later withdrawal from the market was due as much to Intel's preference at the time to concentrate on the higher-priced microprocessor market that Intel then dominated as it was due to the pricing pressures from the Japanese.

February 1971— Intel formally introduced its next big product at the International Solid State Circuit Conference in Philadelphia. This product was an EPROM (erasable, programmable read-only memory). The chip was named the 1702a and would become the forerunner of another huge market in the electronics industry. Intel would also eventually drop this chip to concentrate on microprocessors, but together with the DRAM, the EPROM would form the basic of Intel's success for many years.

February 1971— Intel delivered the first working 4004 and associated chips to fully implement the intended circuit function to its customer, Busicom (*see entry for* October 1969). The first "computer on a chip," the microprocessor, had been turned from an idea into a working circuit. The 4004 was formally introduced and advertised as a "revolutionary product" in November 1971, but no revolution occurred then. However, Intel had already decided to go ahead with the next microprocessor, the 8008. The 8008 project would produce working chips one year later in August 1972.

October 1971— Intel made its initial public offering (IPO) of stock to raise cash and make Intel a public company. Bob Noyce and Gordon Moore were the largest stockholders, holding about 37 percent of the company between them. At the offering price of $23.50 per share, their holdings were worth about $20 million. It was also from this date onward that Andy Grove began to become "more equal than other equals" in the operation of the company.

March 1972—Ray Tomlinson of BBN, the company that had the contract to build the ARPANET, wrote the first fundamental "e-mail" programs. Users of the ARPANET (which would have 29 nodes by October 1972) had been exchanging messages from time to time, and were ready for a more formalized system. The users originally called e-mail "net notes" or simply "mail." Now messages could be sent from computer to computer and placed in a "mailbox" for later retrieval. Modifications were made to the program as time went on and more computers were added to the network.

The "e-mail" feature became extremely popular, and many credit it for the ultimately overwhelming success of the ARPANET. E-mail was instantaneous and it did not require that the sender and receiver be available at the same time. The system was easy to use, and addresses were relatively easy to find. A sender could send a message to several people at the same time, and responses usually came no longer than overnight. Regular mail via the post office soon became "snail mail," and an additional advantage over regular mail and telephone calls (beyond not requiring both people to be available at the same time) was the fact that e-mail was essentially free. Before long, e-mail eclipsed all other uses of the ARPANET in terms of computer traffic.

It was credited for playing a big role in getting users to like the networking sharing process, and the use of e-mail on the Internet today can be traced to another feature of the ARPANET that simply evolved as people learned how to use it. No one planned for e-mail as a feature that would become extremely popular. It simply happened.

June 1972— The Corning Glass team announced that they had made further developments in their glass processing and had reduced the glass loss to four decibels per kilometer. This was nearly 30 times better than the breakthrough they had announced about two years earlier. In addition, the fiber was much less brittle and could be easily drawn from a furnace onto a roll of other fibers. Plans began to be made at telephone companies everywhere to consider fiber optics more seriously.

August 1972— Intel announced its second microprocessor product, the 8008. It soon added an associated product, the Intellec 4, to make the 8008 easier to use. This time the glimmer of a "revolution" began to flicker in the minds of computer designers. Many began to recognize the potential of microprocessors in designing computers.

October 1972— The first public demonstration of the ARPANET was made at the International Conference on Computer Communications (ICCC) in Washington, D.C. This very successful demonstration, together with the growing use of e-mail as described in the entry for March 1972, marked a change in "tone" for the ARPANET. Initially intended as a method for sharing expensive computer resources, networking was now seen as a method of bringing people together. These people were beginning to see that instead of a computing system, ARPANET was a communications system. Its key resource was not huge, expensive computers; its key resource was people.

Networks that followed ARPANET would be designed from the start to act as a communications medium. By the end of 1972, ARPANET was well on its way to turning into the Internet, even if it had not been originally planned as such a network.

March 1973— The first ARPANET international connection was made to the University College of London in England, and to NORSAR (the Royal Radar Establishment) in Norway. It was not realized at the time, but this was a step towards making what would become the Internet an international phenomenon.

April 3, 1973— Martin Cooper of Motorola is credited with making the first portable personal cellular call on this date on a wireless "brick" weighing about 30 ounces. It was nothing like the cell phones of today (which can weigh as little as three ounces), but it was a big step in creating the cell phone industry as we know it now. Eventually cell phones would become tiny computers using land antennas and even satellites to permit calls to be made from anyplace to anyplace in the world.

Cooper's call was not the first "cell phone" call in the United States. That honor belonged to AT&T as described in the entry for January 1969. Cooper did make the first cell phone call on a portable cellular phone.

May 1973— Bob Metcalfe, a Harvard Ph.D. candidate who had been involved in the ARPANET during a part-time job at MIT, created what became known as the Ethernet. This was a method of connecting networks together, which allowed random access to the network. Metcalfe went on to found the 3Com company in 1979, which prospered by giving owners of small computers a way to create local computer networks inexpensively. These systems became known as Local Area Networks (LANs), and they spread around the world.

October 17, 1973— Motorola filed a patent for a cellular phone system based on Dr. Cooper's work described in the entry for April 3, 1973. The patent was granted on September 16, 1975, about a year after AT&T was granted a patent on their version of a cellular phone system. It would take nearly two decades before effective cellular systems were common in the United States and the number of cell phone subscribers would pass one million.

April 1974— Intel began shipping its new microprocessor, the 8080. Its selling price was $360 each, a wry sort of joke on the name of the famous IBM computer series, the 360 mainframe. Intel was now on a roll. It had introduced the DRAM (*see entry for* October 1970), then the EPROM (*see entry for* February 1971), and a line of microprocessors (*see entry for* October 1969) topped by the 8080. It was the fifth-largest maker of integrated circuits, with annual sales of $134 million. Andy Grove had become executive vice-president and was acknowledged to be effectively running the company. More good days were ahead.

May 1974— A paper written by Robert Kahn and Vint Cerf titled "A Protocol for Packet Network Interconnection" describes the first internetworking protocol (known as TCP). The "Internet" on which everyone was working was a way to interconnect several other networks, mainly in the military, with the ARPANET. The term evolved easily into simply "the Internet."

January 1975— The issue of *Popular Electronics* for this month featured the new Altair computer kit on the cover. Only a few people knew the computer shown on the cover was essentially an empty box because Railway Express lost the original computer built for the cover picture. The Altair computer had been designed and built by Ed Roberts, who founded a company called Micro Instrumentation Telemetry Systems (MITS) in 1968. Roberts had almost gone bankrupt trying to compete with Texas Instruments and others in what became a cutthroat electronic calculator business in the early 1970s. Roberts had decided a "minicomputer" could be built around the newest Intel microprocessor, the 8080. *Popular Electronics* was looking for a cover feature to scoop rival publication *Radio Electronics*. There was a feeling in the industry that computers could be sold in decent quantities to electronic and software hobbyists, but no one was sure and the larger established companies hesitated to make a commitment. The Altair kit answered the question resoundingly. It became a runaway success at the price of $397. Although orders poured in, not many shipments were made until the summer of 1975 as the tiny company could barely find time to open the mail.

February 1975— Paul Allen and Bill Gates, eventual founders of Microsoft Corporation, put together a presentation for Allen to give to MITS in Albuquerque showing how Allen and Gates could write a software program to put BASIC (a computer language) on the Altair computer.

Allen and Gates, friends since high school in Seattle, were in Boston when the January 1975 issue of *Popular Electronics* appeared on the newsstands. Allen was working for Honeywell, Inc., in Boston, and Gates was a freshman at Harvard. The two friends had already founded a company called Traf-O-Data in their days in Seattle, featuring a product that would record traffic in a given area to support traffic density studies. Both were "computer nerds," and already had a long history of writing computer software together. Allen was just two years older than his freshman friend, but had already given up on college life and was working in computers in an industrial setting.

Allen saw the cover story about the Altair while walking through Harvard Square, suggested to Gates that they propose to MITS to write BASIC for the Altair (both had worked in BASIC before), and the two entrepreneurs ultimately sold MITS on their efforts.

March 1975— Paul Allen was offered a job as the director of software at MITS. He took the job as he felt it was one of great promise in a field in which he wanted to work. It turned out that Allen himself was the entire software department at MITS. Bill Gates later joined Allen in Albuquerque, and by July 1975 Allen and Gates renamed their company "Microsoft." It would grow into one of the largest and most powerful companies in the world.

The company's first real sale was a licensing agreement for BASIC that they signed with MITS.

March 5, 1975 — The "Amateur Computers Users Group," later better known as the "Homebrew Computer Club," was founded in Menlo Park, California, a suburban town not far from Stanford University in Palo Alto, on the northern border of the Silicon Valley. Attendance at meetings rather quickly grew to more than 750 hobbyists interested in computers. Among the attendees were Steven Jobs and Steve Wozniak, who would go on to found Apple Computer.

April 16, 1975 — A computer enthusiast named Steve Dompier gave a report on MITS and the Altair computer to the Homebrew Computer Club. Dompier had taken the trouble to fly to Albuquerque, New Mexico, where MITS was located and the Altair was being built, when Dompier was unable to get everything he wanted when he ordered an Altair.

Dompier reported correctly than MITS was a tiny company in a tiny building next to a laundromat in a shopping center. The company was buried in orders and didn't even have all the parts it advertised as add-ons. For the hobbyists' club the good news was the fact that there were 4,000 orders. The club members had been longing for computers of their own to work with, and the huge backlog of orders was proof that a demand existed. One way or another, they would be sure to get a computer in the near future.

June 1975 — A company called Laser Diode Labs first offered a commercially available semiconductor laser that transmitted a continuous-wave signal at room temperature. These were gallium-arsenide lasers and were guaranteed to have a lifetime of 10,000 hours. That represented well over a year of testing (the standard thousand-hour test took 42 days), but higher temperature tests were run and projected to longer lifetime. This product announcement marked a milestone in demonstrating that the room-temperature semiconductor laser was not just a laboratory device but also a readily available commercial product. Industry efforts increased to find better semiconductor lasers, and telephone companies like Bell Telephone began to think of field tests of fiber-optic communication systems.

June 15, 1975 — The first meeting of the Southern California Computer Society was held in Miraleste, California. An attendee at the meeting, systems analyst Dick Heiser, noticed that all the attendees were planning to buy or had bought a new Altair computer. He heard that many hobbyists were having trouble assembling the computer and getting it to work properly. The computers often needed additional add-ons such as extra memory boards and disk drives. He was struck with the thought that he could build a business selling both the computer and associated parts as well as help and advice in getting everything set up and working. Two months later he had signed a contract with Altair and opened his retail outlet, ultimately called "The Computer Store." Another new industry, personal computing retailing, had been started, and it would grow along with the personal computer industry. As usual, each industry would feed off the other.

July 1, 1975— The Defense Communications Agency (DCA) took over management of the ARPANET. This was part of a plan to expand the use of networking within the military; DCA was responsible for providing communications services for the entire armed forces, not just ARPA. Seven years later DCA would split military applications from the ARPANET, clearing the way for the ARPANET to become what we now know as the Internet.

August 1, 1975— Wayne Green, who had been publishing a magazine called *73* for ham radio enthusiasts, published the first edition of *Byte* magazine on this date. The magazine was aimed at the same computer enthusiasts who were interested in personal computers, and it was an instant success. *Byte* marked the formation of a new magazine genre, and many other magazines aimed at the personal computer industry would follow in its wake. In the same way as the software industry that was just beginning to grow, the personal computer magazine industry would grow along with the personal computer industry, and one would feed the growth of the other.

December 8, 1975— Paul Terrell decided to move into the new field of personal computer retailing, and he opened the "Byte Shop" on this date in Mountain View, California, in the heart of the Silicon Valley. This was the second notable store in this field (*see entry for* June 15, 1975), and the Byte Shop soon expanded into a franchise operation. By November 1977, there were 74 Byte stores operating in 15 states and Japan, and Terrell sold out. Personal computer retailing was by then an established fact.

January 1976— Ed Faber, a former IBM employee, joined a new company called IMSAI Manufacturing. Bill Millard and Bruce Van Atta had founded IMSAI in early 1975 in San Leandro, California. IMSAI was just beginning production of a new minicomputer intended for use by small businesses rather than hobbyists. Faber was hired to lead the sales team to sell the new computer. In a sense his hiring marked the movement of IMSAI from planning to actually doing.

IMSAI was building its new computer around the same Intel 8080 microprocessor initially used by Altair, but its construction quality was much better than Altair's. In another year about 50 hardware companies would be started to address the minicomputer business. IMSAI would start pushing Altair for the number-one spot in the business, and IMSAI would eventually become number one.

January 13, 1976— The Bell Telephone Company started a fiber-optics communication test system in Atlanta, Georgia. They basically turned it on and then waited for problems to develop. Very few problems appeared over the next few months, and most of those problems had to do with semiconductor laser lifetimes. This was not felt to be a key problem as semiconductor diode laser lifetimes were improving rapidly in the industry (including at Bell Laboratories), and Bell was developing back-up transmitters using light-emitting diodes (LEDs). Thus, if the only problem to be solved with fiber-optic communications turned out to be a need for improvements in the transmitting light source, it was felt this problem could be relatively easily addressed. The Atlanta test was considered a success, and plans were set in motion to try tests in systems that were actually operating.

February 3, 1976— Bill Gates wrote a famous letter on this date complaining about the tendency of computer hobbyists and their friends to steal computer software. He pointed out that no software writer could make a fair wage if everyone stole the software by creating their own software from a friend's copy rather than buying a copy of their own. Gates was primarily addressing copies of BASIC used to run the Altair, and most hobbyists felt that program should come with the computer and had no compunction about "stealing" a copy. This issue of "piracy" would exist for a long time, but as computer users became less technical, and used software applications for a specific task, many users could not duplicate copies as easily and the majority bought their software.

April 1, 1976— On April Fool's Day 1976, Steve Jobs and Steve Wozniak founded a personal computer company called Apple Computer. Few know today that the company had a third co-founder named Ron Wayne, who signed up for a 10 percent interest in the company. As things later grew very frenetic at the company, Wayne asked to leave and Jobs bought out his interest for $500 in only a few months. Apple would be the first personal computer company to really make it big, with Steve Wozniak primarily providing the technical skills and Steve Jobs providing the chutzpah, promotion, and marketing skills. Both men would become multi-millionaires from the venture, although this was several years in the future. Many people date the beginning of the personal computer market from the birth of Apple, but actually the market was in place and ready to explode when Apple was formed.

However, there is no doubt Apple lit the match to launch a new industry with the founding of the company and the release of the Apple I computer.

By the end of the summer, Apple had sold 50 Apple I computers to Paul Terrell, creator of the Byte Shop (*see entry for* December 8, 1975). Eventually the company would sell about 200 of the Apple I computers at the superstitious price of $666.66 each. Steve Wozniak had already started work on the Apple II.

August 1976— Hobbyist John Dilkes staged what was called the "Personal Computer Festival" in Atlantic City, New Jersey. This was the first national personal computer show, and it is generally credited with popularizing the term "personal computer" as opposed to "hobby computing" or "micro computing."

September 21, 1976— A combination computer store/sales representative was launched on this date by Ed Faber of IMSAI computers. The company was ultimately called ComputerLand, and its pilot store was opened in Haywood, California, in November 1976. In less than six years, ComputerLand had 458 stores in its string of franchises.

October 1976— Mike Markkula, an ex-Intel executive who had retired in his early thirties thanks to valuable stock options from Intel, met with Steve Jobs and Steve Wozniak to consider an aggressive business plan for both Apple Computer as a company and the new Apple II computer. Over the next few months, Markkula decided to invest $250,000 of his own money in the company, and he and the two Steves each became one-third owners of a company suddenly worth about $300,000. Steve Wozniak wasn't interested in the business details and only wanted to build computers. Steve Jobs was a true evangelist and wanted to build a big company. It was Jobs who started the string of inquires that led to Markkula, and it was Jobs who kept pushing to make Apple Computer a big company — but at the time even Jobs could not imagine how big Apple would become.

October 1976— A group of computer software writers in suburban Atlanta, Georgia, who had formed an organization called the Computersystem Center in December 1975 to sell Altair computers, called a meeting of other dealers on this date to discuss the possibilities of buying software for the Altair computer from the Atlanta group. A man named Ron Roberts was the leader of the software group, and he eventually formed Peachtree Software (named after a street in Atlanta), which became one of the biggest software companies on the East Coast as the computer industry grew. It was an example of the mutual growth of the software and hardware business in the personal computer industry as described in the entry for Christmas 1976.

Christmas 1976—A computer programmer named Michael Shayer finished a software program called the "Electric Pencil." It was the first word-processing program written for personal computers. The "Pencil," as it came to be called, was very popular, and Shayer ultimately wrote over 78 versions to fit all the existing "microcomputers," terminals, and printers. Shayer finally grew tired of the program because he wanted to spend his time as a computer "tinkerer" and not as a businessman. Much more complex versions of word processors and other software programs would later be developed, as software programs and personal computers grew up as an iterative industry. It hadn't been planned that way, but Shayer was really the first to write a useful software program for non-technical computer users. It was one of those ideas that seem completely obvious in retrospect, but at the time software programs were primarily intended to be used by people who knew their way around computers. The success of Shayer's program led to both the sale of more personal computers and the writing of more programs to permit non-technical people to make good use of those computers. Two mutually beneficial industries were essentially born together.

March 1977—The Federal Communications Commission (FCC) granted AT&T permission to operate a trial cellular phone system that had been begun in 1975. The demonstration system would take place in Chicago. By the mid- and late-1970s Japanese companies were operating cellular systems in Japan, and AT&T opted to use Japanese cell phones to cut the costs of their demonstration system in Chicago. The demonstration went well enough to give an additional boost to the nascent cellular phone business in the United States. Improvements in systems and cell phones made the cellular phone business a great success by the 1990s.

April 1, 1977—Bell Telephone installed a fiber-optic communication system in its Chicago operating system. Fiber-optic cables were threaded through ducts carrying existing telephone lines, and test signals were sent through the fiber-optic cables with no problems. In its careful methodical way, Bell Telephone planned to carry live traffic as of May 11 and make a major press announcement of the feat. Bell turned out to be scooped by a rival telephone company, General Telephone and Electronics, the nation's second-biggest telephone company (*see entry for* April 22, 1977). Bell lost a race (but only for bragging rights) it didn't even know it was in.

April 1977—The first West Coast Computer Faire was held in San Francisco. It was held over a weekend and twice as many people attended as expected. The Apple II computer was shown for the first time and was a big hit at a price of $1298. The Commodore PET was also shown, priced at only

$795, but it was not promoted as aggressively as the Apple II. The personal computer era was coming of age. Apple Computer took advantage of the moment and pushed hard to popularize the Apple II. It was the first personal computer made specifically to sell in large quantities, and the rest of 1977 was a "golden age" for Apple. Dealers were insistent on getting the new computer, and investors came calling to try to get a piece of the new company. By the end of the year, Apple was making a profit and doubling production of the Apple II every three to four months. The company had to move into a new, larger building. The company and its computer were the talk of the industry.

April 22, 1977 — The General Telephone and Electronics Company (GT&E) announced it had carried live telephone-system traffic on its route between Long Beach, California, and its suburban Artesia line. Thus, GT&E became the first company in the United States to send telephone calls via fiber optics. However, when Bell Telephone opened its Chicago line to regular traffic on May 11, 1977, after its April 1, 1977, test run, Bell Telephone carried a dramatically larger amount of traffic than GT&E had done in its live run.

May 22, 1977 — Ed Roberts sold MITS to Pertec, a company making disk and tape drives for minicomputers and mainframe computers. The deal was essentially a stock swap, but it marked the end of MITS and the Altair computer, the first real entrant into the personal computer business. There would be many more to come, but Altair can claim to be first.

There was an associated problem with the deal: Microsoft, the company founded by Paul Allen and Bill Gates, insisted that the MITS software belonged to Microsoft. Microsoft won their point in a legal arbitration, but Pertec went ahead with the deal anyway. With MITS gone, there was no longer any reason for Microsoft to stay in Albuquerque; the company moved to Bellevue, Washington. Bellevue was near Seattle and was where Paul Allen and Bill Gates had grown up. From there, Microsoft would grow into the "900-pound gorilla" of the software business with the young Bill Gates taking over as president of the company.

June 29, 1977 — The Bell Telephone Laboratories announced that it had completed one million hours (100 years) of extrapolated lifetime for semiconductor diode lasers. The diode lasers were thus considered proven for use in future telephone systems, including cables under the oceans.

August 1977 — Jim Warren, editor of the computer magazine *Dr. Dobbs Journal*, and key sponsor of the West Coast Computer Faire, estimated that there were "50,000 or more general-purpose digital computers in private ownership for personal use." Still, although there were almost countless computer clubs, computer magazines and newsletters, there were also hundreds of small computer companies, many housed in garages, supplying those thousands of computers for personal use. No company to date had had the resources and the carefully designed product to fully capitalize on those thousands of buyers, but it appeared that Apple Computer might become the one company to bet on.

September 1977— The Radio Shack Corporation began selling the TRS-80 personal computer it had announced the month before in the Warwick Hotel in New York City. Radio Shack was a hesitant entrant into this field because the company was not sure it could successfully sell a product that seemed to need more customer service and "hand-holding" than its standard products. The TRS-80 was also a completed computer in a box, not a kit that required careful assembly. The company cautiously projected sales of 3,000 units annually, but through the first full month of sales in this September, they sold over 10,000 units. The Radio Shack TRS-80 was the first entry by what could be called "corporate America" into the personal computer business and it was a successful one. Others were to follow.

March 1978— The second West Coast Computer Faire was held. This time the booth space for exhibitors was sold out months in advance. This Faire was held in San Jose, California, near the southern end of the Silicon Valley. The second Faire was again a great success, and the man who had created a company just to put on the Faires, Jim Warren, decided to do one every year. It later became too big for him to manage, and he sold the company to a larger enterprise that continued the Faires, which became important in the growth of the personal computer business.

June 1978— Apple Computer began shipping a disk drive complete with a newly designed printed circuit board that would properly control the drive. Steve Wozniak had designed the drive over his Christmas vacation, just in time for a consumer electronics show held in January 1978 in Las Vegas, and had completed the PC board afterwards. Disk drives permitted data to be stored on a so-called "floppy" disk instead of cassette tapes, and greatly increased the utility of the Apple II. The disk drive also made it much easier to use software packages being developed by the growing software industry.

June 1978— Intel introduced its newest microprocessor named the 8086. This was actually a "stopgap" chip intended primarily to give Intel a product

in the marketplace between the 8080 that had been introduced in April 1974
and a yet-to-be completed microprocessor tentatively named the 8800 that
was intended to be a dramatic improvement in the state of the art in microprocessors (it would be actually called the iAXP432 when introduced in 1981,
and would not be a notable success). The 8086 that was introduced on this
date was intended to compete with anticipated new microprocessors due out
from competitors Motorola and Zilog. However, a cheaper version of the
8086 called the 8088 ended up in the new personal computer announced
by IBM in August 1981, and thus the "stopgap" chip became a much more
significant part of Intel's microprocessor business than was originally anticipated.

October 1978— IMSAI began laying off employees as the company's
emphasis on sales at the expense of all other matters began to affect sales because
customers were unable to get support on either technical or documentation
problems. By the spring of 1979 IMSAI had to file for Chapter 11 bankruptcy,
and in the fall IMSAI was dead. Some previous service employees bought
the company's supplies and tools and started a new IMSAI repairing all the
computers the company had out in the field. In that sense, IMSAI came back
to life, but in essence the second-leading company in what would become
the personal computer business was now defunct.

September 30, 1979— This date marked the end of the third fiscal year
for Apple Computer. Sales of the Apple II for fiscal year 1979 amounted to
35,100 units, more than quadruple the number of units sold in 1978. In 1980,
sales would continue sharply upward, doubling to 78,000 units. Apple was
now the leading personal computer company, having overtaken Radio Shack
and its TRS-80 computer (*see entry for* September 1977). Apple wanted to
be ready for its next product offering, and was planning to introduce an
Apple III at the May 1980 National Computer Conference in Anaheim, California. However, Apple would stub its toe for the first time due to problems encountered with the Apple III.

October 1979— VisiCalc, a computer software "spreadsheet" calculation
program, written by Dan Fylstra and Dan Bricklin, was released this month.
The program was an immediate success. It began at a sales level of 500 copies
a month, and by 1981 it was selling 12,000 copies per month. It was originally written for the Apple II, and it soon became hard to tell whether the
software program sold well because the computer was selling well, or vice-
versa. There was no doubt that the two items had a symbiotic relationship,
as did the entire personal computer and personal computer software industries.

December 1979 — Steve Jobs took his second in-depth tour of Xerox "PARC," the research center installed near Stanford University by the Xerox Corporation. Jobs had taken an initial tour the month before, after he arranged for Xerox to be permitted to invest in Apple Computer in exchange for the in-depth tours. Jobs was deeply impressed by what he saw. Xerox PARC was famous for its advances in engineering development, but Xerox was never able to get a good personal computer to the marketplace. Jobs decided to implement much of what he saw at Xerox PARC into Apple's line of computers. He wanted to use the graphical user interface (GUI) he saw there, and he also wanted to use the "icons" shown on the computer screen and used in conjunction with what was called a "mouse." All of these items and more would eventually appear in the Macintosh computer built by Apple, but they owed their existence to the tours Jobs took at Xerox PARC. Jobs did not get the technical details needed to add these features from Xerox, he got the vision of what the personal computer could become. In future years, many PARC engineers would move to Apple to get the chance to turn their ideas into a product that could make a real impact in the market.

July 1980 — Bill Gates, head of Microsoft, and Steve Ballmer, whom Gates had installed as assistant to the president of Microsoft (Gates) but who was effectively acting as president, came to work one day in unusual clothing: both were wearing a suit and tie, for a meeting with representatives from IBM. The IBM representatives were from its special plant in Boca Raton, Florida, where IBM was rumored to be building its entry into the personal computer market. There was a second meeting a month later where IBM revealed they were in fact planning to build a personal computer (it was known as "Project Chess" (PC) inside IBM). Gates signed a consulting contract with IBM, and started helping them design their new machine and its software. That August 1980 contract would launch Microsoft on its way to being the top company in its field.

Summer 1980 — Tim Berners-Lee created a program called "Enquire." The name was taken from a reference book titled *Enquire Within upon Everything* he used to read in his parents' library when he was a child in England. The purpose of the Enquire program was to find information relating to certain programs being conducted at the Particle Physics Laboratory in Geneva known as CERN. (The organization was originally called the Conseil Européen pour la Recherche Nucléaire, but its name and activities changed and it became known simply as CERN, which is no longer regarded as an acronym.) Berners-Lee was at CERN at that time for only a brief six-month consulting period, and when he left CERN to return to England, he left his Enquire program behind for any other interested person to use. It ultimately was lost, but within another decade Berners-Lee at CERN would name a descendant of that program "the World Wide Web," and it would eventually spread around the globe.

Fall 1980— The Apple III computer was initially released and soon ran into performance problems in the field. Computers were returned to dealers and Apple's reputation suffered badly. By January 1981 most of the defects had been identified and fixes were planned, and the Apple III was reintroduced in late 1981 and sold well. Though Apple Computer as a company had lost some of its sheen, it continued to prosper as sales of the Apple II remained strong.

November 6, 1980— Microsoft finally signed a contract with IBM to provide the operating system, MS-DOS, for IBM's upcoming personal computer. Microsoft also got permission to sell MS-DOS to other customers. This was the deal that essentially "made" Microsoft. They would make money on both the IBM personal computer and sales of their software to others. With Gates' urging, IBM had agreed to make their computer with an "open" system meaning that anyone could write software applications for the machine. The stage was set for IBM to make its big splash the world of personal computers in August 1981, and to make Microsoft's fortune as well.

November 7, 1980— The Apple Computer Company registered with the Securities and Exchange Commission on this date for an initial public stock offering. When the public offering was complete about a month later, Steve Jobs and his co-owners each received nearly $100 million. Apple had succeeded beyond their wildest dreams, but problems loomed immediately ahead.

January 1981— The Osborne Computer Company filed for incorporation. Adam Osborne had decided to build a portable personal computer (many persons called it "luggable" rather than portable). The Osborne computer was introduced at the West Coast Computer Faire three months later in April 1981, and it was the hit of the show. The computer cost $1,795, which was nearly equal to the cost of the included software if the software were purchased separately. The Osborne was projected to sell 10,000 units in its first full year, but before long it reached a peak of 10,000 units a month. The Osborne was a clear success in its first year. However, the personal computer market quickly became very competitive, Osborne management made a classical error in the timing of an announcement for a planned improved model which immediately short-circuited sales of the existing model, and almost as quickly as the Osborne came to prominence, it went downhill. By September

1983 Osborne was bankrupt, only 29 months after making its big introductory splash.

July 1, 1981— Microsoft converted from a partnership to a stock company. Bill Gates, Paul Allen, and Steve Ballmer were the key players. Bill Gates was clearly at the top with 53 percent of the stock, while Allen had 31 percent and Ballmer 8 percent. An initial public offering was not made until March 1985. By then, Gates had 45 percent ownership of the company, which was worth just over $300 million. It would continue to grow.

August 12, 1981— The world's top computer company, IBM, known for its huge mainframe computers, announced its entry into the personal computer market with the IBM PC. As noted before, Microsoft was hired to write MS-DOS, which was the operating system for the IBM personal computer. This launched Microsoft on its journey to becoming largest software company in the world. At the same time, the Intel 8088 microprocessor, also as noted before, was chosen as the key chip in the IBM PC. Thus, both Microsoft and Intel were given huge boosts towards becoming the largest and most dominant companies in their business areas. In only a few years, Microsoft and Intel would become more important factors in the personal computer business than the computer makers themselves.

The IBM PC, priced at $2880, quickly became the standard for the industry, and many people set to work to build and sell peripheral products. In less than six months, 3Com offered Ethernet networking (*see entry for* May 1973) so that owners of IBM PCs could build Local Area Networks (LANs). The IBM PC was a great success and other PC makers were drawn into the market. Between August and December 1981, IBM sold 13,533 of its PCs. In the next two years they would sell a half-million. The personal computer was on its way to becoming a commodity with IBM in the lead. Many within IBM saw the PC as an eventual threat to its mainframe business, but PCs of all types would ultimately erode the mainframe business, and for the moment IBM was on top of the PC business as well.

Summer 1981— Three Texas Instruments employees decided to create a company named Compaq Computer. They decided to make it a "portable" computer, although the final product weighed 28 pounds and was as usual more "luggable" than portable. More importantly, they had some key circuits developed independently that would make their computer an exact "clone" of the IBM PC. This meant that the Compaq computer would run any software program the IBM PC would run. Now the key distinction in IBM-type computers would be price and convenience of use. With the price of a basic IBM PC coming in around three thousand dollars, Compaq had plenty of room to cut the price of its computer while still offering a machine that would run the majority of the same programs as the IBM PC. The Compaq computer was a smash success.

Compaq Computer had $111 million in sales in its first year, an all-time record. Dozens of other companies entered the "clone" business, the most notable of which was Dell Computer, started in 1984 by Michael Dell in his college dormitory room. Dell grew to sales of $250 million in five years, and ultimately came to dominate the computer business using a simple mail-order process. From that time forward, personal computers were nearly as easy to buy as stereos or any other mail-order electronic component.

November 13, 1981— Microsoft held what would become its traditional fall annual meeting. This was a very upbeat meeting, as sales had climbed to about $15 million for the year. A more significant development at this time was the fact that Charles Simony, head of Microsoft's application department, proposed that Microsoft issue its own versions of a spreadsheet, a word-processing program, an e-mail program, and a computer-assisted design (CAD) program. Eventually Microsoft's Excel spreadsheet and Word word-processing program grew out of this effort. Now Microsoft would benefit from growing sales of its "application" software as well as its computer operating system software.

January 8, 1982— An antitrust lawsuit against AT&T, which had been going on for 13 years, was finally settled in favor of the U.S. Justice Department on this date. AT&T was forced to divest itself of its 22 Bell System operating companies. In return, AT&T got the right to enter the computer business, which ultimately turned out to be of minor benefit. The key issue was that the previously closed telephone communications market was now open to competition, and many small companies sprang up to address that market.

March 1982— Among other chips, Intel introduced a new chip named the 80286. It was later called simply the "286" and was one of the first microprocessors to contain more than 100,000 transistors (the 286 had 120,000 transistors). It became the basis for the IBM PC AT (the "AT" stood for "advanced technology"). The 286 would become the launching pad for a whole new line of microprocessor products that would solidify Intel's position as the leading chip company in the world.

June 1982— The Computer Science NETwork (CSNET) built by a collaboration of computer scientists became operational in this month. CSNET was meant to provide university scientists who had no access to ARPANET the same kind of networking services — especially e-mail. The addition of universities to the networking process brought the final Internet one step closer. Vint Cerf provided the new network with technical advice, and the National Science Foundation (NSF) provided more than $5 million in seed money and supported the new network financially until members' dues made it self-supporting in 1985. The NSF would become key to the implementation of a civilian Internet in the 1980s.

October 4, 1982 — This date could be loosely taken as the birth date of the Internet, although as pointed out before the Internet evolved from a number of networking steps and would continue to evolve up to the present day. On this date it was announced by the Defense Communications Agency (DCA) that the agency would split the so-called MILNET (military network) from the ARPANET. The MILNET would take care of military communications, with suitable encryption devices to control who could access their network and what could be said on it. The ARPANET would continue to focus on academic users, developing and testing new network technologies, and stressing open access.

It would take until April 4, 1983, to make the actual split, and even longer to work out all the bugs. The evolution of the Internet into civilian control went step-by-step, as had the entire process of designing it and building it.

December 1982 — A company called MCI Corporation, which had been challenging the long-distance telephone monopoly of AT&T for much of the 13-year antitrust case against AT&T (*see entry for* January 8, 1982), announced it had leased the railroad right-of-way between New York and Washington held by Amtrak, and was going to build a high-technology fiber-optic telephone system. MCI ordered 100,000 kilometers (over 60,000 miles) of the best fiber-optic material from Corning Glass, giving Corning a chance to cash in on its years of outstanding development work.

MCI stated that its system would carry data 50 percent faster than AT&T's, and would need repeaters (amplifiers) only every 30 kilometers (19 miles), which was four times better than AT&T's. It was a time in which AT&T was vulnerable to the attack by MCI. The technical performance of AT&T was hampered by their long-time insistence on doing everything in their own Bell Telephone Laboratories (which had not fully used the breakthroughs at Corning Glass with whom they had a working agreement) because of what the industry called the NIH factor (Not Invented Here). From a business standpoint the entire Bell Telephone Company was in turmoil because of the antitrust decision in January. Most industry observers felt AT&T deserved to lose the case because of its monopolistic practices and its many years of arrogance as number one (Bell Telephone was about a year away from actually starting to divest itself of many of its operating companies).

This date marked a turning point in the telephone business in both the United States and the rest of the world. The big contract MCI had given Corning Glass emboldened the glass company to bring patent infringement suits against competitors and even customers who had been violating Corning patents. The subsequent break-up of AT&T ultimately brought other telephone companies, like Sprint, into the market, and MCI embarked on an ambitious expansion plan. The mid- and late-1980s would become a golden time for fiber-optic communication systems, and the fuse to that growth was lit in this month in 1982.

December 31, 1982— *Time* magazine named the IBM PC as the "Machine of the Year" for 1982. It was the first time that the magazine named a machine rather than a person as "the most significant force" in the year's news. The story in the magazine added other quotes to the effect that "what networks of railways, highways, and canals were in another age, networks of telecommunications, information, and computerization are today." It was already being widely recognized that the new key to communications was the personal computer.

May 1983— This was the month that Phillipe Kahn founded Borland Corporation. It became one of the big players in the creation of software, which became a prime business in the 1980s following the birth of the IBM personal computer in 1981. Earlier software programs that had become very popular included VisiCalc, a "spreadsheet" calculation program released in the spring of 1979, and WordStar, a word-processing program released in mid-1979. After Borland was formed, the software business soon spawned companies that became empires on their own.

Larry Ellison started a small company in June 1977 that grew into the dominant Oracle Corporation in the 1980s. George Tate and Hal Lashlee formed Ashton-Tate in 1980 and created the very popular dBase II program. In April 1982, Mitch Kapor's Lotus Development Corporation produced Lotus 1-2-3, an integrated software program whose primary use was in spreadsheet programs. By the late 1980s, Microsoft, Lotus, and Ashton-Tate were the big three of the software business, and in 1986 the *Washington Post* called the three companies the "GM, Ford, and Toyota" of software producers. Only Microsoft would continue as a dominant software company into the 1990s, with the other companies being absorbed (Borland bought Aston-Tate in 1991 and IBM bought Lotus in 1995). It is important to note that the growth of the software business exploded together with that of the personal computer business: the growth of one fed the other.

September 13, 1983— The Osborn Computer Company declared bankruptcy less than 30 months after it sold its first unit and rocketed into public notice (*see entry for* January 1981). It was one of the most thoroughly analyzed failures in the brief history of the personal computer industry. There was the normal story of too much debt accumulated in trying to catch up with Apple and IBM. The immediate cause of failure seemed to be that Osborne announced its Osborn II (at a higher price) and stopped offering the Osborn I while it was still selling well. Sales suddenly stopped while people waited for the new, improved unit. The Osborn II was too high-priced, the Osborn I was instantly rendered obsolete, and those who were willing to continue with the Osborn I couldn't get one. The company essentially imploded.

The last ironic note was that when the employees arrived on what became the last day, they were instructed to go home without being paid. Guards were posted to be sure no Osborn property was removed, but no one told the guards that Osborn made **portable** computers. Many ex-employees left carrying Osborn's remaining inventory with them.

November 1, 1983— IBM announced its new computer, the PCjr. This was one of the four new computers IBM would create in 1983 in an attempt to broaden its product line in the personal computer area. The PCjr. was intended for the home computer market and was built with cheaper components with less capability than, and at about half the price of, the basic IBM PC (later models were sold at half of even that price). Although IBM eventually sold over a half-million of the machines, it was not considered a success. IBM (and others) had misread the home computer market. People wanted "real" computers, not "toys."

IBM also introduced the PC XT, the 3270 PC, and the PC XT Model 3270 in 1983, but none of these was a spectacular success on the order of the original IBM PC. IBM "clones" were moving into the marketplace, and IBM was still learning what customers wanted in a desktop personal computer.

November 1983— A computer scientist named Paul Mockapetris from the University of Southern California Information Sciences Institute proposed a way of naming "domains" to make it easier for computers to send e-mail on the Internet. Users had agreed to divide Internet name spaces into smaller "domains" for this purpose. Mockapetris developed a "domain name system" that was accepted by users during the 1980s and remains valid to this day.

The basic sites were .edu (education), .gov (government), .mil (military), .com (commercial), .org (other organizations), and .net (other networks).

Other names were added as time went on. In a way typical of the Internet, each host would control the names under a domain name. For example, a host university under .edu would decide how to define sub-names and how many to add. There was no central authority to go through and no one would have to keep track of the names except the host. This ease of control made it easy to join and use the Internet. By 1984, there were 1,000 hosts on the Internet. That number grew to 10,000 by 1987, 100,000 by 1989, and one million by 1992. The growth continues.

November 1983 — At the fall Comdex computer convention in Las Vegas, Microsoft announced it was planning to come out with a new computer operating system named "Windows." This system would have an advanced GUI (graphical user interface), although it would still be MS-DOS at heart. Potential customers did not know at the time that it would be two years later — November 1985 — before any Windows software would actually be shipped. However, the impending presence of Windows would help to convince designers to stick with the IBM/Microsoft MS-DOS approach when considering new computer and software designs.

January 1, 1984 — AT&T underwent its first actual divestiture resulting from its loss in the antitrust suit (*see entry for* January 8, 1982) when it split off its seven regional operating companies. AT&T kept its right to its long-distance transmission capability and equipment manufacture, but it was soon in competition with companies like MCI (*see entry for* December 1982). Competition of this type fueled the market for fiber-optic communication systems because they have much more bandwidth than the old AT&T systems.

January 24, 1984 — Apple Computer introduced its Macintosh computer to do battle with IBM. This was the computer developed by a team led by Steve Jobs after he visited Xerox PARC in 1979 (*see entry for* December 1979). The Macintosh received accolades for its technical features, but after an initial rush, it did not sell as well as had been projected. Jobs had essentially bet the company on the Macintosh, and early in 1985 Apple Computer had its first quarterly loss ever. The stage was set for an upheaval at Apple.

August 14, 1984 — IBM introduced its IBM PC/AT. This computer, based on the new Intel 286 microprocessor, gained many plaudits as a truly advanced personal computer. There were problems with faulty components from suppliers, and IBM was unable to keep up with demand, but the machine showed IBM was serious about the personal computer market and was still able to produce state-of-the-art products.

September 1984— Tim Berners-Lee returned to CERN in Geneva. He began to re-create his Enquire program (*see entry for* Summer 1980), and as his planned stay this time was longer than his previous visit in 1980, he undertook to try to build an information/research documentation program in more depth than he had tried previously. He wanted to incorporate suggestions made as long ago as 1945, when Vannevar Bush, former dean of engineering at MIT who had been head of the U.S. Office of Scientific Research during World War II, had written an article in the *Atlantic Monthly* titled "As We May Think." The article was about an electronic/mechanical machine called the Memex, which would be binarily coded to make and follow crossreferences among microfilm documents using a process similar to how the brain was thought to work.

A computer researcher named Ted Nelson, who in 1965 wrote of "literary machines," computers that would enable people to write and publish in a new nonlinear format called "hypertext," also influenced Berners-Lee. Berners-Lee was further impressed with the contributions of Doug Englebart, who used a "mouse" in a demonstration in 1968, a decade before Xerox PARC featured the mouse concept and 15 years before it was used in the Apple Macintosh computer. The "point-and-click" simplicity of the mouse was something else Berners-Lee wanted to include in his program.

It should be noted that Berners-Lee did not "invent" the Internet or the "browser," nor did he have a "vision" that led him to the "World Wide Web." He simply worked away at his desired documentation system, and— in his words— a process of "accretion" of knowledge rather than a single flash of insight led him to his final system. It was similar to the process of the development of the Internet that had been going on for three decades and was finally coming to fruition at the time Berners-Lee was working in Geneva. As he said, "I happened to come along with time, and the right interest and inclination, after hypertext and the Internet had come of age. The task left to me was to marry them together."

December 31, 1984— IBM reported that its PC sales had grown from $43 million in 1981, the year the original IBM PC was introduced, to more than $4 billion in 1984. The division making IBM personal computers would rank 79th in the *Fortune* 500 if it were a separate company. It would also be the third-largest computer company in the country behind IBM itself and Digital Equipment Corporation (DEC). No other company in the history of the *Fortune* 500 had ever risen so far in so brief a time. IBM's entry into personal computers had been a great success, and in 1984 IBM was estimated to have 63 percent of the personal computer market (the share would drop to an estimated 38 percent by 1987 as IBM "clones" grabbed bigger shares of the market).

May 24, 1985— In an emergency board meeting held on this date, president John Scully of Apple Computer ousted Steve Jobs from a leadership position at Apple. Each man wanted the other removed, and the board of directors backed Scully. Jobs was understandably bitter, but his mercurial leadership was considered no longer suitable for Apple, and Jobs quit the company by September and sold all his stock.

May 24, 1985— A company called Quantum Computer Services was incorporated in Delaware. The company's first on-line service, called "Q-Link," was launched about six months later for the Commodore computer. In 1991 the company would change its name to America Online or AOL.

October 24, 1985— Microsoft was given a license by Apple for the Macintosh operating system. Microsoft had threatened to stop developing programs for the Macintosh, and Apple did not want this to happen. Microsoft was developing their Windows system that they had announced in November 1983 and would actually start shipping in November 1985. Microsoft did not want Apple to sue over the similarity between its Windows program and its associated graphical user interface (GUI) and that of the Macintosh. Apple granted the license to Microsoft with some misgivings, and as it turned out the Microsoft Windows program would be a crucial element in the ongoing growth of Microsoft.

November 1985— Microsoft began shipping Windows 1.0, the program they had announced with great fanfare in November 1983. It was the first of an ongoing series of Windows programs that would come to dominate the computer software industry.

January 1986— Apple Computer brought out the Mac Plus that greatly improved the original Macintosh. With some other new products, Apple Computer got well into the black again, and Apple was on its way to being a $10 billion company.

March 13, 1986— Microsoft's IPO (Initial Public Offering) was made on this date. There was a frenzy on Wall Street to buy the stock. The stock opened at $21 per share and closed at $27.75, with 3.5 million shares traded. At the end of the day, Bill Gates was worth over $311 million, Paul Allen over $177 million, and Steve Ballmer over $47 million. As high as they seemed at the time, these numbers would later seem trifling.

October 1986— Compaq Computer introduced its new computer at the Comdex trade show. Compaq was an IBM "clone" in the sense that it could run the same popular software programs that ran on the IBM computer. However, Compaq had "reversed-engineered" a critical IBM circuit and could thus build its own Compaq computer without infringing on the design of the IBM computer. The portable Compaq was so popular that the company had sales of $111 million in its first year, a record for any American company in history (*see entry for* Summer 1981).

The launch of the new 1986 Compaq computer, which was based on the Intel 386 microprocessor that had been introduced in 1985 and that included 275,000 transistors per chip, was a turning point in the history of the computer industry. It marked the first time that a "clone" had taken a position of technical leadership. The Compaq computer again used a microprocessor from Intel and operating software from Microsoft. From this point Intel and Microsoft, the key players in the underlying processor technology and operating systems, would be the primary guides in the development of the personal computer business. IBM would remain important, but it would be just one of many entrants in the industry, and all the entrants would go where the technology of Intel and Microsoft would take them.

Dell Computer, started as PC's Limited by 19-year-old Michael Dell in his college dormitory room, became an industry leader by selling IBM clones via mail order. By 1986, Dell had $70 million in sales and was on its way to the eventual top spot in personal computer sales.

October 30, 1986— Commercial service began on a fiber-optic cable buried under the English Channel between London and Belgium. There were already 23 cables in that area carrying just over 23,000 voice circuits. The first fiber-optic cable carried 11,500 voice circuits on its own, and carried digital transmissions as well. This was essentially the start of the fiber-optic cable business under the oceans of the world.

December 1988— The first transatlantic fiber-optic cable between the United States and Europe, TAT-8, began service on this date. The TAT-8 fiber-optic cable had nominally nine times as much capacity as the coaxial TAT-7 cable laid in 1983. The TAT-7 cable would be the last coaxial cable laid under an ocean. In 1989 fiber-optic cables would run under the Pacific Ocean between the United States mainland and Hawaii, with branches going on to Australia and Japan. By 1991 there was a TAT-9 carrying traffic from North America to France and Spain. TAT-10 and TAT-11 would follow. Fiber-optic cables were now connecting the world and giving serious competition to satellites. Intelsat, the international telecommunications satellite organization, was forced to cut rates to compete. Fiber optics were now an established and often preferable type of worldwide communications.

March 1989— As suggested by his boss, Tim Berners-Lee made a proposal within CERN to develop his new information-retrieval system. As is typical of many large bureaucracies, he did not receive an official answer. He had generated enough support, however, from several interested internal groups that he could go ahead working on the system on his own.

April 1989— Intel launched its newest microprocessor called the 486. This unit went over one million transistors per chip with a mark of 1,180,000. It was also the last microprocessor to carry a number. From then on, Intel would name its new microprocessors with a protected trademark, the "Pentium." This change also eventually led to the very successful "Intel Inside" marketing plan agreed to by an overwhelming majority of the approximately 1200 companies building personal computers by the early 1990s.

February 4, 1990— Cisco Systems became a public company. Cisco was formed in 1983, and its prime product was called a "router." These devices were connected at the "gateways" between two or more networks, and they directed the packets being switched along the networks to the best paths for these packets to travel. Since packets were the basis for the development of the ARPANET and thence the Internet, not to mention smaller Local Area Networks (LANs), Cisco products were a key part of the growth of the Internet and the many smaller networks made possible by the growth of personal computers.

Cisco is perhaps the best example of the almost irrational desire on the part of the public to own stocks that had anything to do with the Internet and personal computers at the end of the twentieth century. By 1998 Cisco had grown to a multi-billion-dollar company in terms of sales, and it employed more than 10,000 people. In late March 2000, its stock capitalization was the highest in the world. However, when the stock-market bubble burst, Cisco lost 80 percent of its market capitalization. Cisco is still a very valuable corporation with good products in a market of very high potential, but its market capitalization now reflects a more sober view of the world.

February 28, 1990— The ARPANET was formally de-commissioned. Its functions were taken over by the NSFNET, the network the NSF (National Science Foundation) had been building since the 1980s. With the NSF in charge, the Internet was totally under civilian control in every sense of the word. By this date, there were more than 100,000 hosts on the Internet, including over 250 non-United States networks (about 20 percent of the total).

May 1990— Tim Berners-Lee re-submitted his proposal for his information-retrieval system, and just as in March 1989, the proposal was shelved somewhere within CERN. Shortly afterward Berners-Lee convinced his boss to buy the new NeXT computer built by the company Steve Jobs had founded after being forced out at Apple Computer (*see entry for* May 24, 1985). The purchase was approved, and Berners-Lee was able to continue working on his project under the concept of an experiment in using the NeXT operating system and "developing environment" at CERN. Berners-Lee thought about a name for his project, and in an attempt to select a name that would reflect his desire to create a system that would encompass a "global" network that would be ever-growing, he came up with "the World Wide Web." He was not able to create much enthusiasm for his system at CERN, but Berners-Lee had enough enthusiasm of his own for his system, and through the end of 1990 he furiously continued writing code and trying to get other people interested in the concept. He would finally succeed in a big way.

May 22, 1990 — Microsoft released Windows 3.0. This can be considered a big day in the history of the company. The program was a technical and financial success, and critics unanimously approved it as a great leap forward. The previous issues of Windows had received very mixed critical reviews. With the subsequent release of its 3.1 update, Windows 3.0 et al. reigned supreme in the industry until the greatly anticipated release of Windows 95 in 1995.

March 1991 — Tim Berners-Lee released his "World Wide Web" program to a limited number of CERN workers. In May some visitors from the Stanford Linear Acceleration Laboratory (SLAC) at Stanford University found the program very attractive and took it back to the United States with them. SLAC started the first "web server" outside of Europe.

August 1991 — Tim Berners-Lee released more details of his program, including most significantly an alt.hypertext system to be used on the Internet. This exposed his system to the academic community using the Internet. This was a watershed event. It triggered a number of new software installations along the Internet. The result was the beginning of the building of the Web in a true "grassroots" fashion in the same way the basic Internet had been built.

October 1991 — Quantum Computer Services changed its name to America Online or AOL. The company would go public five months later on March 19, 1992.

December 1991 — A conference called Hypertext '91 was held in San Antonio, Texas. Tim Berners-Lee and a colleague set up a demonstration of their World Wide Web program. There were posters above each demonstration booth noting what was being demonstrated. Only the Berners-Lee booth along a specific wall said anything about the Web. At the same show two years later, every project on the equivalent wall was about the World Wide Web.

June 9, 1992— The Internet reached a total of one million hosts on this date. The growth of the Internet was boosted by the passage of the High Performance Computing Act in the United States during 1991, and a 1992 amendment to the National Science Foundation Act of 1950.

June 1992— Tests done using wavelength division multiplexing (WDM) and appropriate optical amplification showed fiber-optic signals could be carried up to 500 miles without standard repeaters. Also, although the basic technology had been around since 1973, use was finally being made of the fact that fibers treated with the metal erbium can amplify signals by themselves at high-enough frequencies. This kind of technological advance would lead to fiber-optic circuits under the Pacific Ocean capable of carrying 600,000 telephone calls at once. Even greater levels of signal density that will propagate even further in glass fibers are now under active development. There is nearly no limit to the developments in optical fiber communications, although once one can carry all of the telephone traffic in the world in a length of fiber that will reach halfway around the world, there is no clear application for additional advances. Present research is going in exactly that direction.

February 1993— The National Center for Supercomputing Applications (NCSA) at the University of Illinois, Champaign-Urbana, made a browser called Mosaic available over the Web. It was created by a student named Marc Andreessen and a staff member named Eric Bina. Berners-Lee had long been pushing for the development of browsers to make it easier for non-technical persons to access the Web. Mosaic would become the basis of the Netscape organization in 1994 (*see entry for* April 1994). Over 40,000 copies of Mosaic were downloaded in the first month, and more than a million copies were estimated to be in use by the spring of 1994.

April 30, 1993— CERN issued a declaration that it agreed to allow anyone to use the Web protocol and code free of charge, and anyone could create a server or browser and give it away or sell it without any royalty or any restraint. This was the ultimate step in turning loose the imagination of users of the Web to create any software item they wished. Before long the browser industry was thriving and big guns like Microsoft would appear in the fray.

June 18, 1993—John Scully left as head of Apple Computer, partially because of burnout and partially because Apple was doing poorly in the face of increased competition. Attempts had been made to sell Apple to larger companies, but no deal came to fruition. The company that really got the personal computer industry into a rapid-growth mode 15 years earlier was now just another struggling computer company.

July 1993—Intel marked its 25th anniversary by announcing sales of about $6 billion and profits of about $1 billion. At the end of the year the board of directors authorized the payment of the first dividend in Intel history. The company was universally acknowledged to be both the biggest and the most important semiconductor company in the world. The previous year the name "Intel" had been designated by marketing analysts as the third most valuable name on earth behind Coca-Cola and Marlboro.

Summer 1993—The number of "hits" on a CERN server maintained by Tim Berners-Lee increased to 10,000 a day. It had been 100 hits a day in the summer of 1991, 1,000 hits a day in the summer of 1992. Berners-Lee realized that the "bobsled" he had been relentlessly pushing was now gaining speed on its track and that it was now time to "jump in and steer."

April 4, 1994—Marc Andreessen, who had helped create a web-browser program called Mosaic the year before while he was still in college, and Jim Clark, founder of the Silicon Graphics company, decided to start a company to sell web-browsers. The company was incorporated on this date and was ultimately named Netscape Communications. Their key product, called Netscape Navigator, would sell 45 million copies by the end of 1996.

April 1994—A business plan was written by an entrepreneur named Jeff Bezos for a company to be called Amazon.com. The company would have its IPO (Initial Public Offering) in 1997, and would become a "poster child" for Internet companies that have stratospheric stock prices and increasing sales without ever turning a profit. However, Amazon.com would do a good job of developing its basic core business of selling books over the Internet, would survive the dot-com stock collapse in 2000, and with many partners for other household products, would become a major Internet retailer.

April 16, 1994—Bill Gates of Microsoft wrote what would become a famous memo to his staff. The memo announced a "sea change," and stated that "Microsoft has decided that the Internet will be very important." He declared that an Internet browser must be included in the upcoming Windows 95, and listed specific tasks for various executives to be sure Microsoft would be adequately addressing the Internet in the future.

May 25, 1994— The first World Wide Web conference was held at CERN. It lasted for three days and attracted about 350 people. The sense of excitement about building the Web for the benefit of the world led reporters to dub the event the "Woodstock of the Web." Among other things, it was agreed consortia would be established in the United States and Europe to oversee the development of protocols and standards for the Web.

August 16, 1994— AOL reached one million members for its Internet on-line services.

September 1, 1994— The Massachusetts Institute of Technology (MIT) had agreed to take on the leadership role for the consortium of the World Wide Web in the United States, and Tim Berners-Lee started work at MIT as a full-time staff member.

November 1994— Microsoft announced that it was launching an Internet access service called the Microsoft Network (MSN), and the software to use it would be part of its forthcoming operating system called Windows 95. This service would compete with America on Line, CompuServe, and Prodigy.

December 1994— Microsoft announced its plans to license browser technology from a small company called Spyglass, formed by engineers previously associated with the development of Mosaic at NCSA at the University of Illinois. The cost was $2 million, but Microsoft was determined to be a big player in the world of the Internet and the World Wide Web. This technology would also be included with Windows 95.

December 14, 1994— The World Wide Web consortium in the United States held its first meeting at MIT. This was the first day of an eventful week for the Web.

December 15, 1994— The day after the first United States Web consortium meeting, Netscape released the commercial version of its browser, now called Navigator. The real significance of the release was that Netscape made it available over the Internet for free. Netscape hoped to become entrenched as *the* web browser, and it initially gained over 95 percent of the market. Its plan was to make money from ads and services it could offer to all those who used its browser. Microsoft was not so easily beaten: it would overtake Navigator in the future.

December 16, 1994— On the third day of this busy week in the history of the Web, CERN announced it no longer intended to serve as the head of the European consortium for the Web. A new construction program at CERN made it impossible for the organization to budget any money to support the Web. France's National Institute for Research in Computer Science and Control near Versailles picked up the responsibility.

January 1995— A company called ICO Global Communications was formed to offer communication services via low-earth-orbit (LEO) satellites (or possibly medium-earth-orbit satellites). LEO systems use relatively cheap satellites that orbit approximately 1000 miles above the earth's surface (or about 6,000 miles in medium earth orbit). They are launched in an orbit that avoids the radiation belts at these levels, and they are very simple satellites compared to those that are meant to provide full-blown communication services in geosynchronous orbit (22,300 miles up). The LEO satellites would provide relatively simple telephone services for "wireless" (mobile or "cell" phones) and Internet and/or data services. LEOs were seen as a new way to achieve low-cost telecommunication services at sea or in countries with minimally developed land services.

February 1995— In Brussels, at the annual meeting of the G7, the world's seven wealthiest nations, the keynote speaker, Thabo Mbeki, the deputy president of South Africa, urged people to seize the new technology of the Web to empower themselves to know the truth about their own economic, political, and cultural circumstances, and to give themselves a voice that the world could hear. It was a clear sign that the Web had indeed become a worldwide phenomenon.

April 1995— The NSF (National Science Foundation) ceased operating the Internet, as it had become a self-operating function. The Internet included 22,000 foreign networks, about 40 percent of the total.

April 1995— Compaq Computer announced that its new line of personal computers would come with Navigator software bundled directly with the hardware. Supposedly Netscape Communications had turned down Microsoft's offer to include its browser on Microsoft's Windows 95 program. Microsoft redoubled its efforts to create its own browser.

May 23, 1995— Sun Microsystems, which had made its fortune in computer workstations, released a new computer language called Java. There were potentially many advantages in the simplicity of this language, but Sun Microsystems planned primarily to use it as a weapon against Microsoft, which

Sun saw as the "enemy." Java would become a consistent controversial topic in the litigation battles that would rage through the end of the century.

July 17, 1995 — IBM announced that its recent purchase of Lotus Corporation would make it possible to make Lotus SmartSuite (and Lotus Notes) IBM's primary program for desk-top computers.

August 9, 1995 — Netscape Communications filed its initial public stock offering (IPO). The stock went from $28 to $71 before it opened, and Netscape, by that measure, was valued at about $4.4 billion by the end of the day. It was the biggest IPO ever to this date. The Internet was becoming an amazing fad, and Netscape Navigator was the most popular way to "surf the net." The price of the stock made no objective sense, but the entire market was booming and Netscape was a "hot" stock.

Most analysts said the "insane" bidding for Netscape was really the first strong public notice of the Internet's potential and marked the beginning of the craze for Internet-related stocks. This validated Bill Gates' comment that the Internet was "the most important single development in the computer industry since the IBM PC was introduced in 1981."

August 24, 1995 — Microsoft released its new Windows 95 program. Windows 95 contained as an "integrated" package the Microsoft browser, Microsoft Explorer. A huge marketing push accompanied the release, including appearances with Jay Leno on television and music by the Rolling Stones. People stood in line at stores for "Midnight Madness": dealers would be open at midnight to officially begin selling the Windows 95 package. Windows 95 was another huge success for Microsoft, selling over seven million copies in two months and giving Microsoft about 90 percent of its market.

October 1995 — Hughes Aircraft was selected to build satellites for the ICO Company that planned to build a low-cost communication system (*see entry for* January 1995). Hughes also contracted to arrange for launch services.

December 7, 1995 — Microsoft held what was called "Internet Strategy Day," at which Bill Gates made what would later be referred to as his "Pearl Harbor Day" speech. Gates said that the Internet was to be "pervasive" in all that Microsoft did. Microsoft would be deeply involved with the Internet and the Web with its own browser, the Microsoft Explorer, which would ultimately be given away for free. The importance of an Internet browser was not only that it gave the user access to the Internet, but also it essentially could eventually be used as the operating system for the computer which was accessing the Internet. Microsoft had negotiated a second deal with Spyglass to license its Mosaic code in order to build versions of the Microsoft browser that would run with other operating systems.

The browser battle was soon joined between Netscape and Microsoft, with other companies including AOL, the leading on-line Internet service, Sun Microsystems, a company that had made its fortune in computer work-stations and had created a new computer language named Java (which Gates announced Microsoft was licensing from Sun), and Oracle joining in as it suited the interest of each company.

December 28, 1995— Following an active year of mergers, AOL service now exceeded 4.5 million members. Serious talks among the players in the Internet browser wars began.

March 12, 1996— AOL announced browser partnerships with Microsoft and Netscape Communications; a licensing and development agreement with Sun Microsystems; and marketing distribution alliances with Apple Computer and AT&T.

May 8, 1996— AOL announced a joint venture to launch an on-line service in Japan. This followed launches in France and Canada earlier in the year. By the end of the month, AOL would have over 6 million members.

January 1997— At an Apple-sponsored conference, Steve Jobs and Steve Wozniak were introduced in partial celebration of the 20th anniversary year of Apple's founding. There was more than anniversary celebrations in the works. Jobs was now a billionaire, having just sold his NeXT company, which he founded after leaving Apple in the mid–1980s, to Apple for $400 million. As well, Jobs was CEO of Pixar, a "hot" company that was starting a revolution in combining computer technology with animated features in the movie industry. Jobs was coming back to Apple as an "advisor," but anyone who knew Jobs predicted he would play a much bigger role than that. Jobs later took over Apple again, and with the help of a $150 million investment from Microsoft (which would then control all of Apple's web browsers), Apple continued as an active part of the computer business.

September 1997— By now Microsoft had managed to capture about 35 percent of the browser market. The company had caused a stir by announcing its plan to integrate its updated browser with its forthcoming Windows 98 operating system. There was a legal issue as to whether the "integrated" approach would violate antitrust laws, compared to the "bundled" approach of including a browser with an operating system. A truly integrated system would give a buyer of Windows 98, for example, no reason to use Netscape's Navigator as a browser.

November 17, 1997 — AOL announced that it had more than 10 million members and that AOL was delivering more daily mail in the form of e-mail and instant messages than the United States Postal Service. In another month AOL members outside the United States would exceed one million.

January 1998 — Netscape announced it would make its entire code for its Navigator browser completely available to the public. This was in essence a desperate attempt by Netscape to fend off the challenge of Microsoft. Netscape hoped enough computer-savvy people would utilize the Netscape browser so they could make any changes they wanted, but most of the public simply wanted a browser they could use at the push of a button or the click of a mouse.

May 18, 1998 — The United States Department of Justice and the attorneys general of some 20 states filed an antitrust suit against Microsoft, alleging that Microsoft had abused its "monopoly" power to thwart competition, especially in the case of Netscape. This suit would drag on for more than five years, and would still be in active litigation as 2004 dawned in the new century. One thing it proved was that Microsoft Explorer had won the browser battle, and the Microsoft MSN Internet portal connection had passed the Netscape Netcenter site in popularity. Microsoft had won the technology battle, but now its key opponent was the antitrust law rather than the technical skills of other companies. Lawsuits and countersuits were common in the software industry, and more than one company had disappeared under the weight of litigation rather than technical problems. Microsoft would ultimately not appear to be seriously damaged by the lawsuit, but lawyers on both sides would enjoy a full-employment status for some time.

July 28, 1998 — Microsoft officially appointed Steve Ballmer as president of the company, and on the same day the company officially launched Windows 98, the successor to Windows 95.

October 19, 1998 — The Microsoft antitrust trial began in Washington, D.C. There were many criticisms of Microsoft's business practices during the trial, and it would end by 2000 in a tentative defeat for Microsoft with the judge recommending that Microsoft be broken up, among other harsh remedies for what he found to be illegal monopolistic behavior by Microsoft. Several books would be written about the trial, with the basic theme that Microsoft had been brought to heel and had been "defeated."

The books were written too quickly. Microsoft appealed, based on both the judge's decisions and his behavior with the media during the trial. Hearings on the appeal would begin in February 2001 and Microsoft would "win" the appeal in June 2001. The original judge was determined to have acted in an improper manner and was barred from hearing further testimony. The break-up order was thrown out, and a new judge was appointed to hear further arguments for other "remedies" for Microsoft's actions. Those hearings would begin in the fall of 2001 and would end in a "victory" for Microsoft. Again there would be appeals, and the case would stagger onward. Still, other than having to make some monetary payments to a number of states, Microsoft would appear to be the victor in the trial by the end of 2001.

November 24, 1998—AOL announced that it had bought Netscape Communications in a stock swap valued at about $4.2 billion. Sun Microsystems was also involved by agreeing to market some Netscape products not needed by AOL in return for giving AOL a cut of the profits from the products and some Sun technology desired by AOL. Netscape essentially disappeared. By the end of the year, AOL membership would exceed 15 million.

Microsoft pointed to the transaction as demonstrating that its so-called "monopoly" position was hardly that and that the Justice Department et al. should drop their lawsuit (*see entry for* May 18, 1998), but the court did not agree and the lawsuit continued.

June 22, 1999—AOL announced a "relationship" with 3Com Corporation to give AOL members access to e-mail via handheld computers. The announcement closed out a month that included the acquisitions of Internet music brands Spinner.com, Winiamp, and SHOUTcast, as well as Digital Marketing Services. Alliances were also formed with Hughes DIRECTV, Philips Electronics, and Network Computer, Inc. AOL was becoming an integral part of the Internet and Internet services throughout the world. By the end of 1999 AOL alone would have over 20 million members for its basic service.

September 18, 1999—Comsat Corporation, the key United States corporation in the history of satellite communications since it was founded by government action in 1962 (*see entry for* August 31, 1962) was acquired on this date by Lockheed Martin Corporation for $2.1 billion. However, the deal would not become final until August 2000 to permit all the necessary government approvals to be finalized. The transaction showed how much the satellite communication business had changed since Comsat was created in 1962. The two big international satellite organizations, Inmarsat and INTELSAT, were also becoming privately held organizations. Inmarsat was privatized on April 15, 1999, and the privatization of INTELSAT was completed in 2001. Satellites were no longer a new and mysterious method of communication, and the fact that they were now relatively routine meant that they could be run in a relatively routine fashion.

November 5, 1999— The judge in the Microsoft antitrust case took the unusual step of releasing his "findings of fact." These findings were devastating to Microsoft, and the findings were released supposedly to give the parties time to settle before the official verdict and resulting "remedies" would be announced. It was obvious from the findings that the remedies would be harsh. However, as noted in the entry for October 19, 1998, a settlement would not be reached; a harsh verdict would be issued in mid-2000; and Microsoft would "win" on appeal in 2001.

January 10, 2000— AOL announced a plan to merge with Time-Warner. AOL shareholders would hold 55 percent of the new company. It would take exactly one year to complete the merger, which would be the largest corporate merger in history, although the value would fall from $166 billion at inception to $106 billion at completion. It would also turn out to be a disastrous venture for the two companies, and the merged company would lose about $200 billion in market capitalization before the merger was partially unwound in 2003.

January 13, 2000— Bill Gates, head of Microsoft, officially gave his close friend Steve Ballmer the title of chief executive officer (CEO) of the company while Gates retained the position of chairman of the board and assumed a new position of chief software architect. The two men had effectively been running Microsoft together for the last 20 years, and this change in titles was not expected to produce any major changes at the company. Their primary problem continued to be the ongoing antitrust battle with the Department of Justice (*see entry for* May 18, 1998). Microsoft still reigned supreme in the world of software used to operate personal computers and access the Internet. Microsoft sales were over $20 billion and its cash on hand was approximately $36 billion. Gates and Ballmer had done very well for Microsoft.

May 2000— ICO Corporation emerged from the bankruptcy protection it sought in August 1999. Cable television pioneer Craig McCaw led a group of international investors in paying $1.2 billion to acquire the company. The first satellite for the company's proposed communication system would be launched in 2001 (*see also entries for* October and January, 1995).

June 7, 2000— Judge Jackson issued his long-awaited decision in the Microsoft antitrust case. He ordered the company broken up, among other remedies for what he determined to be Microsoft's "abuse" of its "monopoly" power. Microsoft appealed the decision, and in 2001 would win a reversal in the court of appeals. Key items would include the removal of Judge Jackson from the case for improper behavior.

December 2000— A company named Iridium Satellite LLC acquired the assets of the former Motorola LEO (low-earth-orbit) Iridium system for $25 million (the Introduction and the entry for January 1995 describe LEO systems). The Iridium system, consisting of a constellation of 74 satellites (66 operating in six interconnected planes plus eight in-orbit spares at a height of about 500 miles) had been a $5 billion gamble by Motorola that it could establish a profitable mobile/cell phone satellite communication system. The Iridium Company had filed for bankruptcy in 1999 about nine months after it was launched. The combination of excess capacity in the satellite industry and some poor business decisions by Motorola doomed Iridium. With no takers for its assets, the bankruptcy judge agreed to permit Motorola to stop spending money controlling the satellites and to let them fall from orbit and be destroyed in the earth's atmosphere. Only a last-minute offer from a group led by entrepreneur Dan Colussy saved the system from destruction. The purchase price amounted to about one-half cent on the original dollar.

January 2, 2001— AOL announced it had set a record for membership growth in a single day by adding more than 70,000 members worldwide on Christmas Day 2000. Earlier in the month, on December 12, 2000, its membership had gone over the 26 million mark for its basic service.

June 28, 2001— The Court of Appeals in Washington, D.C., issued a unanimous 7–0 decision in favor of Microsoft in the antitrust case against it. The case was sent back to the lower courts to reconsider remedies against Microsoft, and the original presiding judge was removed from the trial for improper behavior. The emergence of a new administration in Washington worked in Microsoft's favor, and the horrific events of September 11, 2001, would make everyone involved anxious to settle the Microsoft case quickly to mitigate any possible damage to what was seen as a now fragile economy following the September 11 attacks.

September 3, 2001— Hewlett-Packard announced plans to acquire Compaq Computer in a stock swap worth about $25 billion (by 2002, the new company would have total revenues of about $57 billion compared to about $83 billion for industry leader IBM). Hewlett-Packard (HP) would own about 64 percent of the new company and Compaq about 36 percent. Carleton "Carly" Fiorina of HP would stay as chairman and CEO of the new company, while Michael Capella, chairman and CEO of Compaq Computer, would become president of the combined company.

The deal would not become legally complete until May 2002, following a bruising proxy fight in March 2002 that was narrowly won by HP stockholders on Fiorina's side of the battle. Today, Dell and HP are at the top of the personal computer market in the United States, with Dell slightly ahead. Third-place IBM ranks far behind in this sector of the market. Compaq had previously bought Digital Equipment Company (DEC) in 1998 for about $9.6 billion, so the top computer hardware and service companies in the United States have essentially been reduced to the "new" Hewlett-Packard, Dell, and IBM (which is still the overall leader in computers and office equipment).

September 28, 2001— The new judge in the Microsoft antitrust case, Colleen Kollar-Kotelly, told both parties that a "prompt end to the litigation" was desirable because of the "recent tragic events" of September 11. Two weeks later she appointed a mediator to expedite a settlement with a target date of November 2, 2001.

October 25, 2001— Microsoft released Windows XP, and shipped over seven million units of its newest Windows program in the next two months. Reviews of the program were ecstatic.

November 2, 2001— A tentative settlement was reached under Judge Colleen Kollar-Kotelly in the rehearing of the Microsoft antitrust case. Microsoft, the Department of Justice, and nine of the remaining state attorneys general agreed to the settlement. Other parties, including nine other attorneys general, disagreed and wanted harsher penalties. The judge thus scheduled additional hearings on the "remedy" phase of the trial. These hearings would drag the suit forward into yet another year.

December 28, 2001— AOL announced its basic service now had over 33 million members.

November 2002— United States District Court Judge Colleen Kollar-Kotelly approved yet again another deal made by the Department of Justice in the Bush administration and Microsoft to settle the long-running antitrust suit against Microsoft. This decision would have ended a suit that had officially started in 1998 (*see entry for* May 18, 1998), but appeals were filed by non-federal entities involved with the suit, so the suit still staggered forward under appeal.

January 2003— Steve Case, chairman of the board of AOL Time Warner, announced he would resign "in the best interests of the company." He was almost immediately replaced by Dick Parsons, previously the chief executive officer of the company. AOL Time Warner later announced it was taking a $45.5 billion quarterly loss to account for the declining value of AOL, thus bringing its total yearly loss to nearly $100 billion, the largest loss ever in corporate history.

Analysts said that although AOL had had an almost unbroken period of growth featuring numerous successful mergers and acquisitions since its birth in 1985, the merger with Time Warner announced in January 2000 was a high-risk endeavor that showed once again that two disparate companies would not necessarily become more successful by merging. In addition, AOL had been facing ever-more-intense competition in its role as a leading provider of access to the Internet.

March 2003— Intel launched a new microprocessor called the Centrino, which contained within the chip the capability to permit laptop computer owners to make wireless connections to the Internet without having to install a special card to do so. The Centrino was the brainchild of Paul Otellini, who is the heir apparent to run Intel when the present CEO, Craig Barrett, reaches the mandatory retirement age of 65 in 2005.

April 2003— ICO Company received court approval to acquire a controlling interest in Globalstar, another company that had hoped to offer LEO satellite communication systems but had fallen on hard times (*see also entries for* May 2000 and January and October 1995).

April 9, 2003— The "Money" section of *USA Today* carried an article noting that the wars in Iraq and Afghanistan had greatly improved the fortunes of the Iridium LEO satellite system (*see entry for* December 2000) and similar systems. Other newspapers carried basically the same story at the time. Requirements for mobile/cell phone and other military communications had grown enormously in the Middle East, and now that Iridium had a much smaller debt load and better equipment, it was forecast to make a profit in 2003. LEO systems, at least those that remained after a spate of bankruptcies, were back in favor.

August 6, 2003— The results of a study published on this date in the *Journal of Neuroscience* showed that the common musical scale of which the familiar "do-re-mi" is a part has not derived over time from numerical ratios based on various harmonies, as physicists and mathematicians have long proposed. Studies of thousands of recordings of more than 500 people representing the eight major dialects of regions of the United States show that people place extra emphasis on the tones that correlate to the notes of the musical scale. The same thing occurs in different cultures using different variations of the musical scale, and in different languages such as French, Mandarin Chinese, and German.

The conclusion was that speech, the first and most universal form of communication among the human species, developed regular patterns of emphasis with which humans were comfortable, and music simply evolved with the same patterns. There is even the possibility that "musical" tone patterns preceded speech, but in this "chicken and egg" question, the researchers thought it was likely that speech came first and music followed.

August 8, 2003 — Howard Rosenberg, the television critic for the *Los Angeles Times* for the previous 25 years, announced his retirement on this date in his final column. Among other things, he pointed out that the technology of the medium now moves forward so fast that it is exceeding our ability to measure it and comment on it. There are so many choices today, and TV is so "panoramic," that there are more good and bad things on television than ever before, leaving it up to the individual viewers to seek out the good things on their own.

August 8, 2003 — The *Los Angeles Times* reported today that the FBI was giving seminars to alert parents about the dangers of the Internet in terms of sexual predators who prowl the Internet looking for teenage (or younger) potential victims. The FBI pointed out in these seminars that just as the Internet gives us great access to the world, it also gives the world great access to us. A recent survey showed that 45 percent of teenagers had profiles posted on the Internet but only 17 percent of parents knew about them. Also, 80 percent of these children had private e-mail lines and only 68 percent of parents were aware of them. Further, about 20 percent of children aged ten through seventeen reported unwanted sexual solicitations, with 25 percent being directed at children younger than 13.

The point was made that children should be encouraged to enjoy the wonders of the Internet, but to avoid problems parents must take the responsibility of being aware of how their children are using the Internet. Like all new wonders of technology, the Internet can be abused by people with undesirable motives.

August 17, 2003 — Kevin Starr, well-known writer about and observer of the California scene, wrote an essay for the *Los Angeles Times* on this date pointing out that the furor over the campaign to recall Governor Gray Davis was not the political circus many had characterized it as, but was rather the emergence of a new dynamic, even a revolution, in governance. The emergence of the Internet and the growth of the "high-speed Internet-connected multimedia culture" that has been associated with it leads to an "unfiltered, rabidly democratic" atmosphere that cannot be controlled at any one point. Future political issues and even candidates are going to be subject to this kind of instant review. The political process is now being speeded up to match the "24/7" culture that has been inspired by access to the Internet.

August 20, 2003— Bloomberg News announced today that the average cable television customer spends about $49.62 per month for that service compared to an average of $48.93 for satellite television service. Spending on cable had increased by 41 percent in the previous five years compared to an 8 percent increase in satellite services as more cable customers opted for expanded services such as video-on-demand and digital television. Satellite television continues to gain in market share, growing to 17 percent of households in 2003 compared to 7 percent in 1998. Cable television market share has fallen to 60 percent compared to 68 percent in 1998.

August 25, 2003— The satellite unit of Boeing announced that 10 partially built satellites would be dusted off and completed for the use of ICO Global Communications. ICO had ordered the satellites in 1995, but lean times in the low-earth-orbit (LEO) satellite/mobile phone business had prevented the completion of the satellites. ICO was hopeful increased military use of wireless communications in Afghanistan and Iraq would trigger a general increase in the wireless telephone business and make the area profitable again. The company hoped that satellite deliveries would begin by 2005 (*see entry for* April 2003 and before as noted there).

September 7, 2003— The *Los Angeles Times* on this date ran an article comparing the multimedia corporate giants after GE reached agreement to take over Vivendi Universal and merge it with GE's existing NBC operations. The top companies in the combined fields of movies, broadcast television, and cable programming were AOL Time Warner (soon to become Time Warner as described in the entry for September 19, 2003) with $41 billion in revenues, followed by (revenues in billions): Walt Disney $25.3, Viacom $24.6, Comcast $21.1, Sony $17.2, News Corporation $15.2, NBC Universal $13, and Hughes Electronics $8.9 (planned to become part of News Corporation in December which would raise News Corporation to position number four at $24.1 billion).

After News Corporation took over Hughes, the top seven companies would have total revenues of $166.3 billion, with NBC Universal last at $13 billion. This is why there are so many mergers in this area: a corporation with "only" $1 billion or less in revenues cannot hope to have much of an impact on the market. GE's challenge would be to greatly expand its holdings and/or acquire more companies.

September 18, 2003— The board of directors at the merged AOL-Time Warner company voted to drop the "AOL" from the company name. It was not clear if any further action would be taken to undo some aspects of the AOL-Time Warner merger that was completed in January 2001, with generally disastrous results (*see entry for* January 2003).

October 16, 2003— Cable operator Cablevision announced today it would offer high-definition satellite television service to compete with Echo-Star and Hughes DirecTV. The service, called Voom, will focus on high-definition television as the preferred format in years to come. The new service is typical of many new ventures in this area, an ambitious system definition with no paying customers as yet.

November 4, 2003— A federal appeals court met again on this date to address the ongoing Microsoft antitrust case. The case had effectively been going on since October 20, 1997, when the Clinton administration claimed Microsoft had violated a previous agreement. When that claim failed, a new antitrust suit was filed in May 1998 (*see entry for* May 18, 1998). The suit had followed an up-and-down course since then, with Microsoft generally being seen as ultimately "winning" the case on appeal. Of the 20 states originally filing suit together with the Justice Department, only Massachusetts was still pursuing the case. The trial judge had basically ruled in favor of ending the case against Microsoft, and only two industry associations and Massachusetts were looking for harsher penalties. The industry associations contained key competitors of Microsoft (AOL, Sun Microsystems, Red Hat, and Oracle) and they were naturally looking to do as much damage to Microsoft as possible. The appeals judges were quoted as being skeptical of the new appeals, and appeared likely to uphold the decision of the lower court. If so, the long-running battle could finally be coming to an end.

November 5, 2003— Intel Corporation announced that it had developed a process that could permit up to one billion transistors to be placed on a single chip. With the present state of the art at about 55 million transistors per chip, the new chip's anticipated production date of about 2007 would keep "Moore's law" (*see entry for* April 19, 1965) essentially intact through at least the first decade of the new century. This continual doubling of the number of transistors per chip that was forecast almost 40 years ago means the computer industry will continue to provide more and more computing power at lower and lower costs, and all semiconductor-based products will provide higher and higher performance as costs continually decline.

November 24, 2003— New federal rules took effect today to permit wireless (cellular) telephone customers to keep the same wireless number if they switched wireless providers. According to a story in the *Los Angeles Times* on this date, it was estimated that as many as one-third of the 152 million cell phone users in the United States could switch providers over the next few years. There were about 179 million wire-line users in the country, and it was further estimated that about one-tenth of them could now move their telephone numbers to wireless service. The companies most affected were Verizon Wireless, the country's largest carrier with 35 million customers, and AT&T Wireless, the second-largest carrier.

November 25, 2003— The United States Senate deferred action on a bill to extend the federal ban on taxing access to the Internet. The ban had been in place since 1998 and was intended to encourage the growth of the Internet. The ban officially expired on November 1, 2003, and some states had passed laws permitting Internet taxes if the moratorium were not extended. The states were anxious to create new sources of tax revenue, and many opponents to extending the moratorium argued the Internet was now well enough established to survive some new taxes. Others argued for no taxes to permit the Internet to grow, especially in the area of high-speed Internet access (about 30 million households now have such service). The Senate is expected to take action one way or another in 2004.

November 28, 2003— The *Los Angeles Times* carried an article today in which the writer, Nick Schulz, responded to a recent article in the *Harvard Business Review* about whether the Internet and information technology (IT) in general had become so ubiquitous that they had become a commodity like electricity: everybody has it and uses it properly so there's no way to gain a competitive edge by creating innovations in either field.

Schulz pointed out that the success of e-Bay in a generally "down" economy, and the surge of Howard Dean among the Democratic presidential contenders, show that the Internet can still make a positive difference when used in an innovative way. Further, almost 40 percent of homes have a wideband connection today (on the way to 80 percent in five years), and this has helped online shopping to grow by 24 percent in the third quarter of 2003 compared to 2002. It is estimated that online sales will top $100 billion in 2003. Starbucks, McDonald's, and Wal-Mart are among the firms that are planning to use wideband Internet connections in their stores. It appears that the Internet will continue to be an ever-growing force in communication, and businesses that are innovative in its use will prosper more than those that are not.

December 12, 2003— An article in the *Los Angeles Times* on this date reported that corporate communication giants AT&T and Time Warner were discussing a plan to send phone calls over the Internet in data packets that would be treated as e-mail by the Internet. Time Warner had previously announced talks with Sprint and WorldCom MCI.

The technique is called "voice over Internet Protocol" or simply "voice over IP." Many active in the field call it VoIP. The technique has been around since 1995, but never found its way into widespread use. However, the Internet is much more lightly regulated than the telephone industry, and using the Internet could avoid access fees, which are about 1.5 cents per minute on long-distance calls and thus add up to about $25 billion a year. With tight competition in the telephone business, the savings could be attractive. Big usage is in the future, but it marks another step towards the Internet's becoming the primary communications tool for all purposes around the world.

December 19, 2003— The Federal Communications Commission (FCC) gave final approval for the takeover of DirecTV (owned by Hughes/GM) by News Corp., owner of Fox Broadcasting as well as many television stations and cable channels (*see entry for* September 7, 2003). This acquisition moved News Corp. up into the top rank of media conglomerates that provide our basic forms of communication outside the Internet. General Motors and News Corp. completed the deal to sell DirecTV to News Corp. on December 23rd.

December 22, 2003— *Time* magazine on this date carried an article describing what it forecast to be an upcoming battle to control the Internet web-search business. Google had been the clear leader to date in this area, where about 550 million Web searches were made daily among the estimated 500 billion documents existing on the Internet. The advertising market involved with these searches is valued at about $2 billion per year. In an area where everyone deals in huge numbers, Google has indexed about four billion web pages to date, but other competitors have passed the three-billion mark. Known names such as Microsoft, Yahoo, and Amazon.com are in the hunt. Amazon.com has scanned every page of 120,000 books, and its customers can scan every page of these books online.

A technique called "paid search" is the present Holy Grail. This essentially involves ads that appear only when searchers have indicated a clear interest in a product through their searches. Revenue in this area is estimated to hit $5.6 billion by 2007. With that amount of money involved, and with the Internet rapidly becoming "the primary means by which people get information about the world," the web-search business is sure to attract many companies in the future.

December 29, 2003— An article in the *Los Angeles Times* points out that Internet online advertising exceeded $6 billion in 2003. This reflects the fact that 140 million Americans are on line, and the fact that online advertising is the preferred method to reach this group. It is forecast that new records will be set in 2004 due to the substantial amount of online advertising that will be associated with the presidential election campaign.

December 31, 2003— Sales of semiconductors, consumer electronics products, and personal computers are all forecast to increase in 2004 compared to 2003, but businesses rather than individual consumers are expected to take the lead, according to market research firms as reported in the *Los Angeles Times* for this date. Worldwide semiconductor sales should reach $197 billion in 2004, the fourth consecutive year of increase but still below the $225 billion reached in 2000. Worldwide personal computer shipments should reach 48.8 million units by the fourth quarter of 2004, continuing their steady growth since 2002. Finally, consumer electronics shipments in the United States should reach $97.3 billion in 2004, a little ahead of its average for the five years from 2000 through 2004. In spite of slowdowns throughout the world in many areas, the insatiable desire of people to communicate and their related desire to own electronic products that help them do so more quickly and more widely continue at relatively strong levels.

December 31, 2003— In a transaction that many did not notice on this last day of the year, package delivery giant FedEx (annual revenues of $23 billion) acquired Kinko's, a specialty chain of copy stores primarily serving small businesses (Kinko's has about 1200 outlets generating around $2 billion in revenue annually). FedEx plans to increase its relationships with the small businesses frequenting Kinko's stores so that FedEx can compete more directly with rival UPS.

　　The unknown story behind the deal is that Kinko's was started in 1970 by college student Paul Orfalea (it takes its name from a nickname for Orfalea and his curly hair). Kinko's grew sharply in the 1980s and is a prime example of the impact of the personal computer and the small businesses that sprouted in that era. Entrepreneurs using their PCs and service companies like Kinko's put themselves into business as almost one-man (or one-woman) enterprises. Kinko's added Internet access as it came along, and it continued to offer services that small businesses could use as a "back office." It could easily be said that Kinko's was a creation of the PC and the many small businesses that the PC permitted to be born. Now it has reached the "big time" as part of FedEx. Founder Orfalea sold out in the 1990s, but his creation is going strong.

January 2004— The "Inside Business" insert in *Time* magazine (dated this date but published in December 2003) carried another article on "VoIP," the technique for making telephone calls over the Internet (*see entry for December 12, 2003*). Telephone systems permitting Internet calls will grow by 80 percent in 2003 to about $1.6 billion. That market will reach over $5 billion in 2007. There will also be an effort made to integrate the many products now being made to make telephone calls and access the Internet into one hand-held unit.

January 7, 2004— The *Los Angeles Times* on this date carried an article showing that in 2003 for the first time there were more women online shoppers than men. For 2003, retail sales online came to $56.2 billion, an increase of 28.8 percent for the year. This type of increase is projected to continue in the years ahead, but it must be noted that even with these strong gains, online shopping accounts for only 3 percent of total retail sales in the United States. This means the majority of shoppers do it conventionally, but it also means there's lots of room for growth online. Also, in a new trend, online shoppers concentrated on home and garden items rather than the consumer electronics (including personal computers) that led the list previously. The Internet has not only become a major facet of communications throughout the world, but it is definitely now a major element in nearly everything we do.

January 7, 2004— According to the *Los Angeles Times* on this date, Intel Corporation, the world's largest semiconductor company, was expected to announce today that it was starting a venture-capital fund to invest in start-up companies developing hardware and software for digital home communication networks. The venture will be called the Digital Home Fund and will have a capitalization of $200 million. It will be the latest in a family of funds under the Intel Capital umbrella, and it reflects Intel's attempt to create new sources of demand for its products by creating companies whose products will be based on Intel's technology. The continuing growth of communications of all types will eventually force much of that communication to take place in digital form, which offers greater capacity.

January 12, 2004— Ivan Seidenberg, chairman and chief executive officer of Verizon Communications, Inc., was quoted in an interview with the *Los Angeles Times* on this date as saying that his company is concentrating on upgrading its land lines and wireless networks so that they will work better together and at higher speeds. This will permit customers to find new ways "to consolidate and manage their phones, hand-held devices, laptops, and other electronic gear."

Nearly all communication companies are heading in this direction, but Verizon, the nation's largest local phone company, and the largest mobile/cell phone carrier with its Verizon Wireless unit, has committed $3 billion to the task. It plans to run fiber-optic cable to more than a million homes this year, but it hopes to sell local calling, long-distance calling, and Internet services without significantly expanding its traditional landline networks. Verizon is an excellent example of how communication services companies must adapt to the various demands by their customers for more and better communications, while doing it with better technology that permits many functions to be combined to provide customers with "one-stop" shopping for their communications needs.

January 14, 2004— Intel Corporation announced that sales for the fourth quarter of 2003 were a record $8.74 billion, and they topped $30 billion for the full year. Intel continued to hold its position as the world's largest chip maker, with microprocessors for computers still its leading business. However, Intel added that its Centrino chip for wireless applications was doing very well, and the company believed that it would benefit from the trend of computer makers seeking new markets in the consumer electronics field as television sets and such things as DVD players required increasing amounts of computer power.

January 22, 2004— Microsoft Corporation, the world's largest software company, announced that sales for the last three months of 2003 exceeded $10 billion. It was the first time sales had reached that level for any three-month period, and sales for the fiscal year ending June 30, 2004, were expected to top $35 billion.

It seems notable that the two companies that essentially control the direction of the personal computer and related products business, Microsoft and Intel, were very nearly the same size (*see entry for* January 14, 2004, regarding Intel) about three decades after each had been founded just before the personal computer had begun its climb to glory. Even more notable was the fact that each company was the biggest in the world in its field.

January 29, 2004— The *Los Angeles Times* reported in an article today that media giant Time Warner had reported a profit for 2003, its first since the disastrous merger with AOL in 2000. AOL, however, continued its downward spiral. The one-time king of the on-line business lost about 830,000 subscribers who either terminated or agreed to receive the service free as part of AOL's desperate attempt to keep from losing subscribers. AOL now has about 24 million subscribers, down dramatically from its peak of over 35 million in 2002. It's yet another example of how quickly circumstances can change in the competitive high-tech world. Analysts expect AOL to continue losing subscribers.

February 1, 2004— An article in the *Los Angeles Times* on this date discussed how the Hewlett-Packard Company (HP) and Apple Computer negotiated a deal in January for HP to sell Apple's iPod digital music player under the HP brand name. This deal is a good illustration of how companies are rising above old images to compete in today's world of consumer electronics and basic communication products: HP, unable to develop a successful digital music product of its own, simply adopts the successful Apple product under the HP name. Most people do not realize that although HP's corporate slogan is "HP invents," the $10 billion line of laser printers sold by HP are made by Canon Corporation.

Similarly, although Apple Computer was the first big leader of the personal computer business, Apple has only 3 percent of the global personal computer market compared with 62 percent of the hard-drive-based music-player market, and more than 70 percent of the legitimate music-downloading market. Further, Apple has had immense success with its Pixar Animation Studios division that reached a peak in 2003 with its film *Finding Nemo*. The studio is looking for other partners now that Pixar has recently decided not to renew its existing deal with Disney. Steve Jobs, head of Apple, will soon be remembered more for computer animation of films and his music industry activities than for being a pioneer of the personal computer business, if he is not in that category already.

February 2, 2004— Intel announced today a new line of computer chips with greatly improved performance. This is an ongoing process for Intel and is a key reason it maintains its rank as the world's leading computer maker. Buried in the announcement was a brief comment that Intel was helping to hold down the costs of the highly complex chips by making them from 12-inch-wide silicon wafers instead of the 8-inch-wide wafers it had been using.

Wafer size is important because the area of the surface of the wafer, where the chips are chemically deposited, increases with the square of the radius, i.e., a two-inch-wide wafer produces four times as many chips as a one-inch-wide wafer. There are other considerations, including the retooling needed to handle bigger wafers, but generally the bigger the wafer the cheaper each chip is on a per-unit basis. When integrated circuits began to be manufactured in the 1960s, the jump from a one-inch wafer to a two-inch wafer was a major advance in the state of the art. Now an increase to a 12-inch wafer from an 8-inch wafer is hardly worth mentioning. The manufacturing capabilities of today are truly breathtaking in the chip business.

February 2, 2004— In an article in the *Los Angeles Times* today, the recent split between the Disney Corporation and Pixar, the computer-animation company headed by Steve Jobs, was analyzed in depth. The article suggested that the basic cause of the dispute between the two companies, whose partnership since 1991 had generally been both artistically and financially successful, was the incompatibility of the leaders of the two companies, Michael Eisner and Steve Jobs. The official reason for the split is that Pixar wanted a bigger piece of the pie in the negotiations held to forge a new deal.

February 5, 2004— The Federal Communications Commission announced today that it planned to decide if a company called Free World Dialup could send telephone voice calls over the Internet without paying what could be millions of dollars to local telephone companies in "routing" fees. The company said it should not have to pay such fees because its service essentially avoids the public telephone system in its use of the Internet. The technique is now often called Internet telephony rather than its prior name of voice over Internet Protocol or VoIP (*see entries for* January 2004 and December 12, 2003). It was anticipated the FCC would rule at its next meeting on February 12, 2004, and that, based on comments from FCC Chairman Michael K. Powell, the ruling would be favorable to Internet telephony in general as well as favorable specifically to Free World Dialup.

February 6, 2004— The Associated Press carried an item today disclosing that Microsoft's associate general counsel Richard J. Wallis would become chairman of the antitrust section of the American Bar Association in the coming summer. An unusual position for a corporate lawyer, it is a reminder of how important legal maneuvering is for the communication giants of today, just as it was in the days of Samuel Morse, Alexander Graham Bell, and the builders of the radio empire of the 1920s. Legal issues have always been key to the building of companies in the United States, no matter what field the companies choose to enter.

February 10, 2004— In a deal yet to be announced, Microsoft and the Disney Corporation agreed on terms today to work together to make digital entertainment more secure and more widely available. The deal was similar to one between Microsoft and Time Warner that was announced last year, and is part of an ongoing effort by Microsoft to get elite movie studios to make more use of its software. The new deal was also expected to be seen as a response by Disney to its recent breaking off with Pixar.

February 11, 2004— It was announced today that Comcast Corporation, the nation's largest cable television operator with over 21 million subscribers, planned to launch a hostile takeover bid for the Walt Disney Company. There was no guarantee the bid would succeed (the approximate value of the deal would be $66 billion if it were consummated), but it demonstrated the growing power of the cable industry. In the last four decades the cable industry has grown from a curiosity to a 300-channel enterprise to which over 70 percent of American households subscribe (not counting the 20 million subscribers to satellite rivals like DirecTV and EchoStar). The cable industry is now a major player in the communication business.

The attraction of Disney to Comcast was Disney's movie library as a source of content for its cable channels, not to mention Disney's own cable channels including ESPN. Comcast hopes to make Disney's ABC network (now derided as the "fourth" network behind CBS, NBC, and Fox) as part of Comcast's digital video-on-demand service. Brian Roberts, head of Comcast, said that "the bottom line is to accelerate the digital future." Whether the Comcast bid succeeds or not, this kind of focus on adding expanding digital services to the options for cable television subscribers is sure to drive similar deals in the months ahead. The future of communications by cable in every form will demand companies with expanded resources in a highly competitive environment.

February 12, 2004— At its regularly scheduled meeting on this date, the Federal Communications Commission (FCC) once again addressed the issue of what is now constantly called Internet telephony, the practice of making telephone calls over the Internet using the voice over Internet Protocol (VoIP —*see entries for* February 5, 2004, et al.). The FCC said it planned to regulate the practice lightly so as not to damage innovation. The FCC also granted Free World Dialup permission to operate its VoIP service without being hampered by stringent (and expensive) telecommunication regulations.

VoIP requires the proper software and microphones of some sort at each end of a computer-to-computer hookup, so it will not become widely used immediately. However, it offers a low-cost approach to regular telephone conversations, and is sure to grow in the future. The FCC action today may be the first baby step in yet another way to communicate.

February 13, 2004— It was reported today that Dell, Inc., still the world's biggest personal computer maker, had sales in 2003 of over $41 billion. According to market research firm IDC, Dell had 16.9 percent of the global personal computer market in 2003 compared to 16.4 percent for its main rival, Hewlett-Packard. All other personal computer makers were well behind in market share in the low- to mid-single-digit range. Dell's chief financial officer Jim Schnieder said Dell's goal still was to reach sales of $60 billion in a few years. Dell has recently aggressively entered the general consumer electronics market to expand beyond its domination of the personal computer market.

February 16, 2004 — In the issue of *Time* magazine carrying this date, there was an article noting that airline carriers like Lufthansa were planning to offer broadband Internet access. The service, named Connexion by its supplier, Boeing, turns the entire airplane into a wi-fi "hot spot." The plane then links with the Internet via a network of satellites. Passengers will be able to surf the Web, download attachments and upload pictures at speeds comparable to a regular cable broadband service. The cost will range from $10 for flights across continents to $30 for a flight around the globe. This continues the trend towards ensuring that no one ever will be unable to access the Internet, regardless of their location.

February 17, 2004 — The Federal Trade Commission (FTC) and the Federal Communications Commission (FCC) jointly won a favorable decision from the Tenth Circuit Court of Appeals in Denver upholding the federal government's "do not call" rule. This rule bans companies who wish to sell products via "tele-marketing" from calling persons who have served notice they do not wish to receive such calls by signing a national "do not call" list (which holders of 56 million phone numbers have already done). This is a clear case in which many persons have decided that less communication of this sort is better.

February 17, 2004 — It was announced today that Cingular Wireless, the second-largest cell phone carrier in the United States, had agreed to spend about $41 billion to purchase AT&T Wireless, the third-largest cell phone carrier. Between them, Cingular and AT&T will have about 45 million subscribers, which will put the new company ahead of the previous number-one carrier, Verizon, which has almost 38 million subscribers. In terms of market share, the new company will have about 30 percent, compared to over 24 percent for Verizon. Some analysts say that Verizon may soon regain its number-one position based on its anticipated rate of growth.

Cingular is about 60 percent owned by SBC Communications, Inc., and 40 percent owned by BellSouth Corporation. Number-one Verizon was not interested in AT&T because of a conflict in the basic technology each company uses to operate its cell phone system.

The other prime bidder for AT&T was the British company Vodaphone Group, which already had a 45 percent stake in top-ranked Verizon, a stake that would have had to be given up for Vodaphone to acquire AT&T. Many Vodaphone investors were unhappy about this idea, and they were happy to see the Vodaphone bid fail.

AT&T had put itself up for sale on January 22, 2004, after a series of poor results convinced the company that the cell phone carrier market was due for a consolidation. Cell phones have been an immense success in the United States and around the world, but the operation of cell phone systems in the United States had become highly competitive and profits were not there for everyone. The new company will continue to be called Cingular and will maintain its headquarters in Atlanta.

Most analysts felt that this consolidation would produce some "breathing space" in the cell phone system market in the United States and thus no more large-scale consolidations were anticipated. There was still the possibility of the merger of smaller companies at the regional level.

February 18, 2004— An article in the *Los Angeles Times* today said that Google, the top search engine on the World Wide Web, has officially announced that it has increased its number of Web pages to about 4.3 billion, an increase of about one billion from its previously announced level of about 3.3 billion (the information behind the entry for December 22, 2003, had speculated that Google had already reached the four-billion level). In addition, Google announced it now had about 880 million Web images compared to its previous level of 400 million.

This announced increase in depth was seen by analysts as an attempt to show Google is staying ahead of competitors Yahoo and Microsoft as Google prepares for an upcoming IPO (Initial Public Offering) later this year. However, in a total market where it is estimated that there are 10 billion pages on the Web, the top search engine can change dramatically over time. As of December 2003, data showed Google's websites handled 35 percent of Web searches while Yahoo had 27 percent and Microsoft had 15 percent.

February 18, 2004— In response to Google's announcement of an increased number of Web pages as noted above, Yahoo said it would no longer use Google as a search engine in the United States. Yahoo had previously paid Google for the right to offer Google's search engine to Yahoo customers. But now Yahoo would use its own technology, and soon spread that worldwide.

Analysts see this as the first blow in a coming war over search engines and the potentially lucrative market of "pay-for-placement" advertising. This technique is discussed in the entry for December 22, 2003. Yahoo is the most-visited portal on the Internet, with 111 million visitors to its websites in January 2004. But Google, with 60 million visitors to its websites in the same month, is the leading search engine, conducting 35 percent of searches compared to 27 percent for Yahoo, as noted in the previous entry.

It is anticipated that Google, Yahoo, and Microsoft will be fighting a pitched battle for search-engine supremacy for some time to come. Bill Gates of Microsoft admitted recently that he had underestimated the importance of search engines, and Microsoft plans to add a search capability to its Windows software so that customers could bypass Google and Yahoo completely. The battle should be fierce.

February 24, 2004— Microsoft announced today that it was implementing a system to try to stem the flow of the "spam" that plagues e-mail users (spam is the term used for unwanted advertisements that clog many e-mail systems). Bill Gates, head of Microsoft, said the system would take a number of years to be effective because everyone would have to use the system to make it work well.

On another front, Microsoft was remaining out of the Comcast-Disney battle even though Microsoft had a significant investment in Comcast. Microsoft has avoided "Hollywood" involvements, although many analysts have pointed out that Microsoft is bound to become involved in the entertainment business whether it wants to or not because most entertainment products are heading for digital techniques, and Microsoft holds a key to enabling digital products to avoid piracy.

March 3, 2004— An article in the *Los Angeles Times* today discussed the intention of the Cinergy Corporation utility to offer high-speed broadband Internet service over its power lines. Customers would access the lines via a special modem that would be plugged into existing electrical outlets in the home. The service, sometimes known as BPL (Broadband over Power Lines), has been often discussed, but Cinergy will be the first large company to attempt to provide it. The attractiveness of the concept is that the many millions of standard power company consumers would only need to plug into their existing power lines without needing professional installers. The Federal Communications Commission (FCC) is looking into rules for the operation of the service, and even though the potential is high in terms of the many consumers having electrical service, conventional providers could still win out by bundling various cable services such as movies, cable access, and telephone service together. Either way, methods for gaining access to the Internet will continue to grow.

March 5, 2004— At the same time the search engine service Yahoo introduced a service called "Site Match" intended to collect more revenue from what is called "paid inclusion" in ads placed in its search mechanisms, "Ask

Jeeves," a competing service, said it was dropping paid inclusion. The *Los Angeles Times* today carried an analysis of the competing viewpoints. Many industry analysts feel paid inclusion contains an inherent conflict of interest, but billions of advertising dollars are at stake. The controversy is expected to intensify.

March 8, 2004— This date marked the beginning of a new retail push to market the Internet telephone service known as VoIP (voice over Internet Protocol). Vonage Holdings is teaming with Circuit City stores to offer Vonage digital phone adapters and two months of VoIP service for $99 to retail customers. More such arrangements are expected in 2004 now that the Federal Communications Commission has approved the VoIP concept.

APPENDIX 1:
THE TECHNOLOGY OF
ELECTRONIC COMMUNICATION

Figure 1 shows how the different parts of the electromagnetic spectrum are used in the process of electronic communication. The lowest frequencies shown in the figure are 15 hertz (cycles per second) to 20,000 hertz, the approximate range of speech/music detectable by the human ear. The next frequency ranges listed, 535 to 1605 kilohertz (535,000 to 1,605,000 hertz), are the frequencies originally shown on the dials of the first AM (amplitude modulated) radios. They represent the frequencies at which each radio station was broadcasting its signal. The information which the original radio broadcasts were carrying was human speech and music. Thus, since the human ear responds to frequencies in the range of 15 to 20,000 hertz as noted above, these are the information frequencies carried by the "carrier waves" of 535 to 1605 kilohertz.

The carrier waves propagate through the atmosphere as electromagnetic energy after being transmitted by the antenna of the radio station. A radio set can detect these waves and separate the information they are carrying from the transmitted wave. The circuitry in the radio then sends that information to the radio speaker so that the listener hears the original voice and musical sounds created in the radio studio. The purpose of the higher frequency carrier-transmitting signal is to transport the information to the radio so that the basic information can be reproduced at that location. The entire frequency spectrum that is used in communication works on this fundamental principle.

145

FIGURE 1

The Electromagnetic Spectrum

Approximate Frequency Range	Typical Usage	Terminology
15–20,000 hertz (20 kHz)	human speech, music	very low frequency (VLF)
535–1,605 kilohertz (1.6 MHz)	AM radio listed on the dial	medium frequency (MF)
3–30 MHz	short wave radio	high frequency (HF)
30–300 MHz	FM radio, VHF television	very high frequency (VHF)
300–3,000 MHz (3 GHz)	UHF television, mobile/cell phones	ultra-high frequency (UHF)
3–30 GHz	radar, microwave relays, satellite communication	super-high frequency (SHF)
30–300 GHz	millimeter wave communication	extremely high frequency (EHF)
1,000 (10^3)–10^4 GHz	photography	infrared radiation
10^5–10^6 GHz	fiber-optic systems, human vision	visible light
10^6–10^8 GHz	sterilization	ultraviolet radiation
10^8–10^9 GHz	medical x-rays	x-ray region
10^{10}–10^{13} GHz	therapeutic cancer treatment	gamma rays
10^{14} GHz and higher	physics and astronomy applications	cosmic rays

Before we discuss the elements of carrier waves and information waves in detail, as well as other aspects of electronic communication by electromagnetic energy, we will work our way down the table shown in Figure 1 as an overview of how the spectrum is used. As noted above, the table begins with the lowest frequencies used to transmit the basic information of speech and music. The entire electromagnetic frequency spectrum runs from zero to infinity, including very low frequencies that we perceive as radiant heat and electric power. Some people can "hear" a wider range of frequencies than others, but generally the lowest frequencies heard are those at the very bottom of a piano keyboard and the highest frequencies heard are those at the top of the keyboard.

As a rough rule of thumb, the transmitting frequency must be about 10 times as high as the frequency range of the information being carried (the "bandwidth"). Thus, when the information being carried is the human voice and musical sounds (roughly 15 hertz to 20 kilohertz), the bandwidth is the full range up to 20 kilohertz. The minimum AM radio transmitting frequency of 535 kilohertz is nearly 30 times as high as the basic information being carried. Thus, all of the frequencies on the radio dial are well above the bandwidth of the frequencies being carried.

If we wish to carry more information, the transmitted frequencies must increase. Further, the wavelengths of each frequency decrease as we move down the table (the wavelength is essentially the speed of light divided by the frequency). There are certain efficiencies that occur in the transmission and reception of signals that have wavelengths close to the physical size of the transmitting and receiving elements. For example, the wavelength of a frequency of one million hertz (one megahertz or 1 MHz or 1,000 kilohertz) is 300 meters or almost a thousand feet. The wavelength for a frequency of 10 billion hertz (10 GHz) is three centimeters or a little over one inch. Thus, if you were building an antenna for flight applications where size and weight were issues, you would prefer a frequency of 10 gigahertz and its wavelength of inches rather than a frequency of one MHz and its wavelength of almost 1,000 feet. This kind of issue, added to the bandwidth issues noted above, produces upward pressure on the frequencies chosen for communication. There are many other considerations, as we will discuss in a moment, but just these two issues drive our frequency choices upward.

As shown in the figure, radio broadcasting started to use the 535–1,605 kHz frequency range. This frequency moved upward to the MHz bands as more information had to be carried, and as techniques were developed to handle higher frequencies. The advent of television required carrying video data as well as audio information, and transmitting frequencies moved up accordingly to the hundreds of MHz. World War II put immense pressure on circuit development and transmitting and receiving techniques, and suddenly operating frequencies shot past 1 GHz (one million hertz) and on into the tens and hundreds of GHz. This brought us radar, various kinds of microwave (so named for the short wavelengths of its operating frequencies) relay systems, and finally mobile phones and satellite communications.

The need for greater information bandwidths to carry more complex signals such as digital data (and/or thousands of telephone conversations rather than just one on the same circuit) produced much work on so-called millimeter frequencies (frequencies approaching 100 GHz where wavelengths are measured in millimeters). It was difficult to transmit and work with these frequencies. Rectangular or circular "tubes" about the size of a thumbnail were needed to transmit these frequencies because they could not be sent reliably through the atmosphere without high losses, and any unusual physical pressure on the wave guides (which had to be buried in practical use) caused distortions in the transmission.

These problems were solved when the laser was invented and methods of making low-loss glass fibers came along nearly at the same time. Now the transmitting or carrier frequencies could be moved up near the frequency of light, which is a part of the electromagnetic spectrum like any other. It just so happens that the human eye responds to these very high frequencies (because the eye developed to respond to sunlight) similar to the way the human ear responds to the very low frequencies of sounds produced by vocal chords or animals crashing through the brush.

Light frequencies are not important for electronic communication because they are "visible," but rather because their very high frequencies permit them to carry a great deal of information. As can be seen in Figure 1, light frequencies, even at the low end of their range in the area of red light, are on the order of ten thousand times higher than the "high" millimeter frequencies used in prior communication experiments. Thus a system consisting of solid-state semiconductor lasers as a transmitter and very clear glass fibers as the medium in which the laser light is propagated by reflection can carry much more information than other means of communication.

Digital data, which has very stringent bandwidth requirements, or hundreds of thousands of telephone calls on the same circuit, can easily be handled by the high operating frequencies of fiber-optic systems. It is not clear whether even higher frequencies can be used for communication purposes. As frequencies increase they become more energetic on a "per unit" basis and even become harmful to life.

Ultraviolet frequencies, those a little higher than "light" frequencies, are often used for sterilization as they kill various forms of bacteria. Above these frequencies come X-rays, whose danger is well known, and then gamma rays and cosmic rays. Gamma rays have been used for cancer treatments because they kill human cells: if they can be directed to kill many cancer cells at the cost of killing relatively few "good" cells, their use can be therapeutic. Cosmic rays are deadly, but in the worlds of fundamental physics and astronomy they can be "used" to learn things about the universe and the atom without exposing anyone to them in a way that would be deleterious.

Before we leave Figure 1 and its comparison of how the electromagnetic spectrum is used in the world of communication, the following items may help in our understanding electronic communication.

In FM radio, which means that the transmitting frequency is "frequency modulated" rather than "amplitude modulated" as is the case for AM, additional information must be carried to enable the signal to be properly decoded by the radio set. Also, the FM transmitting frequencies must avoid interfering with AM frequencies, so FM transmitting frequencies are set higher in the range of tens to hundreds of megahertz. Television signals also require more bandwidth for the complex information they carry, and thus television broadcast signals also are moved up to the megahertz range. As the transmitting frequencies become higher and higher, it is easier to separate them so that one signal will not interfere with another.

As discussed previously, higher frequencies have many advantages including the ability to carry more information. However, in the early days it was difficult to build circuits and components that would generate, detect, and process higher-frequency signals. Thus, the lower the frequency the more easily it was adapted for use. As more information had to be carried, higher frequency capabilities were developed in an almost iterative fashion. This is why reading down the list of frequencies in Figure 1 is almost like reading the chronological history of electronic communications.

As noted, amplitude modulation (AM) means that the magnitude of the signal being transmitted is "modulated" by the signal of the information being carried by electronically impressing the information signal upon the carrier. Environmental phenomena like thunder and operating machinery and various obstacles in the transmission path will also "modulate" the amplitude of the signal being transmitted. Such "modulation" will be heard as "static." Frequency modulation or FM uses transmitting circuitry that modulates or changes the frequency being transmitted. Such a signal is not affected by items that modulate the amplitude of the signal. Thus "static" is avoided. That is why FM radio was expected to replace AM radio, but for a number of reasons (discussed in the text) it did not do so.

The modern equivalent of this comparison is the transmission of data digitally where the signal is either present or not present in the form of a "one" or "zero." The absolute magnitude of the signal is not critical beyond a certain "threshold" level. Thus, digital transmission is "better" than conventional or analog transmission. It also permits much more information to be received accurately because there are far fewer "error" signals.

Radio signals at the lower frequencies can "bounce" off the atmosphere, especially at night, and thus can travel a long distance, although not reliably. Signals at higher frequencies, such as those used for FM radio and television, travel more or less in a straight line and will continue off the earth into outer space: they travel only to the horizon. That is why many early transmitting stations were located on high places such as the Empire State Building in New York City to extend the "view" of the "horizon."

APPENDIX 2:
THE CELL-PHONE EXPLOSION

Figure 2 shows the growth of cell-phone subscribers in the United States since 1985. In that year, there were only 385,000 cell-phone subscribers in a total population of about 235 million people, or about 1.6 subscribers per 1,000 people. Portable cell phones had been invented in the early 1970s, but it took almost two decades to improve both the cell phones and cellular phone systems to the point where people began to use them in significant numbers.

By 1990, there were over 5 million subscribers in a population of over 248 million, a subscriber rate of over 21 subscribers per 1,000 people. In the 1990s many improvements were made to cell phones, making them much smaller, cheaper, and easier to use. At the same time, in an iterative fashion, adults began to find cell phones advantageous to keep in touch with their offices and their homes. Children in their teens and younger also found cell phones very useful in their incessant "need" to communicate with their peers. Parents, working and otherwise, found cell phones a simple way to keep in touch with their children in a world increasingly dangerous for children.

As a result, by 2000, there were over 100 million cell-phone subscribers in the nation, meaning the subscriber rate was up to 400 subscribers per 1,000 people. Continued improvements in cell phones, including their ability to reach greater distances via LEO satellite systems, have continued to increase the demand. As of 2002, the most recent year good data was readily available, cell-phone subscribers had increased to over 140 million in the United States, producing a subscriber rate of 490 subscribers per 1,000 people.

This means that the subscriber rate for cell phones has increased from

FIGURE 2

Growth of United States Cell-Phone Subscribers

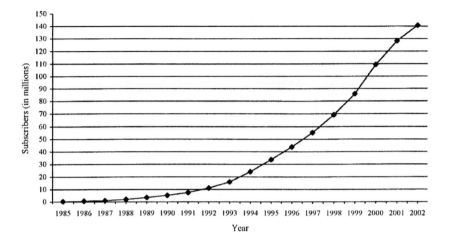

Year	Subscribers (in millions)
1985	0.4
1986	0.7
1987	1.2
1988	2.1
1989	3.5
1990	5.3
1991	7.6
1992	11.1
1993	16.0
1994	24.1
1995	33.8
1996	44.0
1997	55.3
1998	69.2
1999	86.0
2000	109.5
2001	128.4
2002	140.8

1.6 people per thousand to almost 500 people per thousand in just 17 years. It can be anticipated that the rate will continue to increase. Although the United States has by far the greatest number of cell-phone subscribers with its total of over 140 million (Japan is second with almost 80 million), the United States ranks far down the list in subscriber rates. Countries such as Taiwan and Luxembourg have subscriber rates over 100 subscribers per 100 people, i.e. they each have more cell-phone subscribers than they have people. To date, about 30 countries have over 70 subscribers per 100 people (over 700 subscribers per 1,000 people), and this number continues to grow.

The subscriber rate in the United States can double its present level and still not reach 100 subscribers per 100 people. There are certainly many people who cannot afford a cell phone, but there are also many groups who account for multiple cell-phone subscribers. The cell phone has to rank as one of the most popular developments of the latter part of the twentieth century, and the phones' use can be predicted to grow even if many people find them irritating and, when improperly used by drivers of vehicles, dangerous.

As with many popular developments that are felt to fill a specific need with great efficiency, people continue to find additional uses for cell phones even as manufacturers continue to add additional features. Further, as discussed below, many underdeveloped countries find it much easier to install a minimal cellular phone system than a full-blown telecommunications system. This gives their citizens the incentive to buy a cell phone that they can put into use immediately, rather than waiting years for a conventional telephone line to be installed. Cell phones are here to stay.

Figure 3 shows the growth of main telephone lines for conventional telephone service compared to the number of cellular subscribers during the 1990s and into the new century, a period when cellular telephone service began to demonstrate explosive growth. As shown in Figure 2, which covers only the United States, cellular phone service grew dramatically in the 1990s as both cellular telephones and cellular telephone systems improved substantially. The United States already had an existing telecommunications system that was the best in the world. Cell phones were just another option, and although their use expanded greatly, cell-phone subscribers never exceeded the number of main telephone lines for conventional phone service.

However, the story was different in the rest of the world. Many countries did not have well-developed telecommunication systems and/or systems that worked reliably and responded quickly to new needs of their customers. Even in countries considered to be well developed, people could wait years for a telephone line to make its way to their home or apartment, or wait a long time for repairs or the addition of new features. In so-called "Third World" countries there were very limited telecommunication services in many areas, especially outside the major metropolitan centers. Satellite services had

FIGURE 3

Worldwide Growth of Cell-Phone Subscribers
Compared to Main Telephone Lines

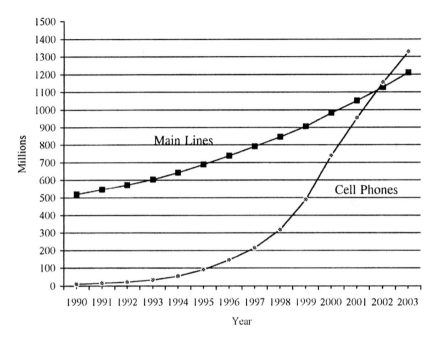

Year	Main Telephone Lines (millions)	Cell Phone Subscribers (millions)	Cell % of Main
1990	520	11	2.1
1991	546	16	2.9
1992	572	23	4.0
1993	604	34	5.6
1994	643	56	8.7
1995	689	91	13.2
1996	738	145	19.6
1997	792	215	27.1
1998	846	318	37.6
1999	905	490	54.1
2000	983	740	75.3
2001	1053	955	90.7
2002	1128	1155	102.0
2003	1210	1329	110.0

been a boon to these countries since large earth stations at least could bring telecommunication services into the country, even if there was a limited infrastructure and no hope of stringing the thousands of miles of telephone wires needed to realize widespread telecommunications services.

Cellular telephone systems changed this picture. They needed only relatively simple towers to be built at certain intervals (although the towers contained sophisticated equipment which had to be bought), and individuals with cell phones had an instant telecommunications service. Thus, in the world as a whole, cell-phone subscribers outnumbered the number of main lines for conventional telephone service by 2002.

In 1990, when Figure 3 begins, the number of cell-phone subscribers in the world came to only two percent of the number of main telephone lines in the world. By 1995, cell-phone subscribers were 13 percent of the number of main telephone lines, and the number of subscribers climbed to 75 percent of the number of main telephone lines by 2000. Finally, by 2002, it was estimated that the number of cell-phone subscribers passed the number of main telephone lines. It is projected that in 2003 the number of cell-phone subscribers will top the number of main lines for conventional telephone service by 10 percent.

The same trend is also taking place in the United States, but most recently the number of cell-phone subscribers was estimated to be over 140 million while the number of main lines for conventional telephone service was still well above this number. It is expected that the number of cell-phone subscribers will eventually pass the number of main telephone lines in the United States as it has in the world at large.

It should also be noted that the number of main lines in the world for conventional telephone service is projected to have grown by over 230 percent between 1990 and 2003. Thus, the number of cell-phone subscribers has been chasing an ever-growing target. This makes the fact that the number of cell-phone subscribers has finally passed the number of main lines for conventional telephone service even more remarkable.

APPENDIX 3:
RADIOTELEGRAPHY
COMPARED TO
RADIOTELEPHONY

There is often much confusion about who invented "radio," and when. Although this issue has been previously addressed, this appendix — explaining the differences between what are often called radiotelegraphy and radiotelephony, and discussing who did what in each field — will make it clear who "invented" radio as we know it now, and when the discovery took place.

The word "radio" in general use was first applied to the development of "wireless" communication as demonstrated by Guglielmo Marconi of Italy in the early and mid-1890s. The word "radio" then had nothing to do with radio as it is now understood, but was rather a term associated with the "waves" that carried communication signals in a "wireless" system, i.e. a system that communicated without the wires used in telegraph and telephone systems.

These waves were not "invented" by anyone. They had been around since the beginning of the universe. The great Scottish physicist, James Clerk Maxwell, postulated their existence in 1873. Based on his study of light, which is just another part of the electromagnetic spectrum as shown in Appendix 1, Maxwell deduced that electromagnetic waves, although mostly invisible, must fill the universe at frequencies ranging from zero up to infinity. He wrote his famous "Maxwell's equations" to describe their behavior, and these equations have been used by physicists and other scientists ever since. This event was really the beginning of "radio," although the word was not used at the time.

The next step in the process was the experiments of German scientist Heinrich Hertz in the late 1880s. Hertz, after whom the unit of frequency was eventually named, showed that the waves postulated by Maxwell actually existed, and Hertz was able to generate and detect them in his laboratory. Future experimenters called the waves "hertzian" or "radio" waves, but Hertz himself pursued his experiments no further. When one of his students asked him what use could be made of the waves, Hertz simply shrugged. When specifically asked if they might be used in communications, Hertz said that such application simply would not work. Hertz died of blood poisoning at the early age of 37 in 1894, and thus he never got a chance to join the extensive work being done with "hertzian" waves in the 1890s.

A prime practitioner of this work was Guglielmo Marconi, the son of a wealthy Italian father who had married a member of the Jameson family of Irish whiskey distillers. This gave Marconi, who was well educated, a private place and the resources to conduct experiments with "radio" waves. Marconi read everything he could find on the experiments of Hertz. After conducting experiments on the grounds of his estate, and developing generation and detection devices, Marconi decided such waves could, in fact, be very useful in the field of communication.

Marconi was only 21 in 1895 when he reached this conclusion. He was unable to interest the Italian government in his work. As a result, he went to England with the help of his mother's contacts and patented his early work in 1896. It was the first of many patents Marconi would receive in his lifetime. Marconi started a company bearing his name; his first customer was the British military which needed communication products for what would become known as the Boer War. After many successful demonstrations of his "wireless" products, Marconi started another company called American Marconi in the United States in 1899 that was allied with his English company. In 1909 he received the Nobel Prize in physics for his work in "wireless telegraphy."

The phrase "wireless telegraphy" reflects a key aspect of Marconi's history. Marconi did not invent nor develop "radio." There were many people active in the wireless communication field at the time, although none were as successful as Marconi. These people are often claimed by their various countries of origin as "inventors" of radio, but they no more invented radio than did Marconi. Marconi, and most of his contemporaries, was working on the wireless transmission of signals based on the telegraph. What they were transmitting was the "dash-dot-dash" of telegraph messages, not the human voices and music of what we now know as radio.

This means that persons such as Édouard Branley of France, Alexander Popoff of Russia, and Nicola Tesla of Croatia did not in any way invent radio. They worked in the field of electricity and wireless communication in the time of Marconi and made various contributions to the field, none of which was the radio. Even a British scientist named Oliver Lodge worked with wireless communication at the time, but he later was to fault himself for giving up on the field, concluding that the telegraph and the telephone were fine as they were. All of these men were working on the wireless transmission of telegraph signals (wireless telegraphy), and Marconi has to be credited with most fully developing the field of wireless communication. Certainly, the patents he received prove at least in a legal sense his mastery of the area.

Other inventors, however, were very much interested in transmitting human speech and music by wireless techniques, even if Marconi was not (and never showed any interest in doing so during his domination of wireless transmission in the first two decades of the century). One of the first "radio broadcasts" was made on Christmas Eve in 1906 by Reginald Fessenden, an American inventor who was active in the wireless field. Using an ordinary microphone derived from the basic telephone, Fessenden modulated a generator of hertzian or radio waves with the sounds of himself singing, playing a violin, and reading from the Bible. He also added music from a phonograph, and "broadcast" all of this from a transmitter located at a site known as Brant Rock on the coast of Massachusetts just south of Boston.

The operators of the wireless communication systems on ships at sea were startled to hear voices and music coming through their earphones rather than the usual mix of static and the dots and dashes of Morse code. The speech and music they were hearing were much distorted, but the sense of the transmission could easily be made out. This event is the first known wireless transmission of telephony, i.e. the transmission of what would normally be transmitted by a telephone system as opposed to a telegraph line. It could be called the first radio broadcast, but it really was an experiment to see if a wireless transmission system could carry such sounds. Except for the microphone, there were basically no electrical components in the system especially intended to carry the sound of human speech and music. That was yet to come — as was "radio."

Lee De Forest provided what would be the next key step in the development of radio. He invented the "Audion" tube in 1906, and by 1907 he was trying to duplicate what Fessenden had done in the 1906 radiotelephony broadcast. De Forest was a tireless inventor who cranked out patents in large numbers, hoping to strike it rich. The Audion was a key invention, but there is clear evidence that De Forest did not understand how it worked. He finally sold rights to AT&T in 1913 for use of the Audion in long-distance telephone circuits. AT&T managed to connect the east and west coasts of the United States via telephone in 1915, using a version of the Audion. De Forest continued his radiotelephony experiments, but they had limited clarity and were little more than ongoing experiments. The outbreak of World War I in 1914 hampered these experiments, and the entry of the United States into the war in 1917 stopped them completely. Radiotelephony was seen as a "toy" interfering with communication developments needed for the war effort.

The appearance of Edwin H. Armstrong on the scene in 1913 was a key turning point in the development of radio. Armstrong understood completely how the Audion tube worked, and he went on to make a number of improvements in the circuitry using the tube. Armstrong developed a number of key concepts that would prove important in radiotelephony, including regeneration, heterodyne operation, and superheterodyne operation. Armstrong would lose a bitter patent battle on regeneration to De Forest in the Supreme Court in the 1930s, but most scientists in the field agreed that in the teens Armstrong made this and other crucial inventions that led to radio broadcasting and the mass production of radio sets in the early 1920s. Armstrong continued to develop circuits when he was in France as part of the American forces sent there for World War I (he became a major and was often called Major Armstrong thereafter). Armstrong later invented FM radio. Edwin Armstrong could easily be credited as the key inventor behind the development of "radio."

However, Armstrong was not the inventor or the developer of radio broadcasting, or the prime mover behind the manufacture of millions of radio sets after 1920. That distinction goes to David Sarnoff, who gained fame as the American Marconi wireless radio operator who was credited with staying at his post for several days receiving messages as the *Titanic* went down in 1914 and other ships broadcast news of survivors afterwards. Sarnoff was the first to conceive of radio broadcasting in the sense of sending wireless telephony into the air essentially at random, to anyone who had a (radio) box to receive the signal. Sarnoff said he proposed such a system to his superiors at American Marconi in 1916. All professional wireless transmissions up to that date had been point-to-point, or at least point-to-intended-point in the case of SOS calls. Nothing came of his proposal, partially because of the entry of the United States into World War I in 1917, and partly because Marconi's company was interested only in wireless telegraphy.

American Marconi was forced to sell its American holdings after World War I because the United States did not want a "foreign power" (Britain) to control such a crucial area as wireless communication. This sale resulted in the creation of the Radio Corporation of America (RCA) in 1919. David Sarnoff ended up at RCA and soon rose to a high-level executive position. He tried once again to sell his radio broadcasting idea, but the crucial elements of his proposed system were bogged down in endless patent litigation. The United States government had declared a patent battle moratorium and arranged for a pool of cross-licensing during the war to permit the United States to have the communications services needed for the war effort.

Sarnoff was given the assignment of untangling this patent mess before launching his radio broadcasting idea and the building of "radio" boxes. While he was so occupied, Westinghouse, one of the key investors and owners of RCA, started radio station KDKA in Pittsburgh in 1920. They simply followed an informal radiotelephony broadcast started by one of their engineers, Frank Conrad, and a department store promotion designed to sell receivers made from kits to listen to Conrad's broadcasts. The success of KDKA and other similar efforts across the United States convinced the powers-that-be that Sarnoff knew what he was talking about. Sarnoff tirelessly promoted various events to attract the public to the concept of radio broadcasting and the purchase of radios to listen to the broadcasts. By 1922 sales of radios were in the millions. RCA prospered both from selling radio sets and collecting royalties on the various patents it held.

Sarnoff would essentially repeat this process with television. The key technical inventions of electronic television were made by Vladimir Zworkin of RCA's research laboratories, and Filo Farnsworth, an independent inventor who dreamed of wealth from his inventions, but who did not have the business skills of David Sarnoff. RCA finally bought patent rights from Farnsworth after yet another bruising court battle, combined Farnsworth's inventions with Zworkin's, and (even before legally owning Farnsworth's rights) announced the dawn of television at the World's Fair of 1939 in New York City. World War II delayed the process, but after the war television sets sold even faster than radio sets had sold 25 years earlier. The key man behind both developments was David Sarnoff, even if he never invented anything — except, perhaps, the most visionary concept of radiotelephony.

Sarnoff had the vision, and acted on it to greater effect than anyone who invented some critical part used in the final system. In this sense, Sarnoff has to be credited as the "Father of Radio" (and the "Father of Television" as well).

APPENDIX 4:
FROM TRANSISTORS
TO INTEGRATED CIRCUITS
TO MICROPROCESSORS

In the field of communications, the transistor has been called the most important invention of the first half of the 20th century, and the microprocessor has been called the most important invention of the second half of the 20th century. Sometimes, the microprocessor has been called the most important invention of the entire 20th century. This appendix is meant to help readers understand, in very simple terms and in one place, what transistors and microprocessors do, and why they and the key invention that links them, the integrated circuit, are so important to the development of communication (and many other fields).

The transistor was invented on December 16, 1947, at the research laboratories of the Bell Telephone Company in Murray Hill, New Jersey. Bell Laboratories did not announce the invention until January 1948 when the holidays were over. Thus, many references specify 1948 as the date of invention. The three men who divide credit for the invention, John Bardeen, Walter Brattain, and William Shockley, were jointly awarded the Nobel Prize in physics in 1956 for their research work on semiconductors and their invention of the transistor.

The fact that the transistor was fabricated from semiconducting materials opened up a brand new field for the development of electrical and electronic components. Electrically, the transistor was the semiconductor equivalent of the three-element vacuum tube, the triode, which had been invented in 1906 by Lee De Forest under the name of the Audion. The triode had been greatly improved since then, and much had been learned about how to use it in electronic applications. The inventions of Edwin H. Armstrong were especially useful here.

A prime advantage of using the semiconductor-based transistor in these applications was that semiconductors worked with operating voltages and currents (amperes or simply amps) expressed in term of millivolts and milliamps, and their power consumption was similarly expressed in terms of milliwatts. Regular vacuum tubes operated at levels of volts and amps and watts, levels a thousand times higher than those of transistors. Also, there was no filament required for the transistor that had to be supplied with energy and allowed to "warm up" to permit the tube to start operating. Transistors were instantly "on" and their lack of a filament eliminated a constant source of failure that plagued vacuum tubes. Because they were so much smaller, lighter, and longer-lived than vacuum tubes, transistors found their way rapidly into all kinds of electronic applications in which they replaced vacuum tubes. This was especially true when their ability to operate at higher frequencies and more rapidly than vacuum tubes when used simply as off-on switches was taken into account.

As noted, transistors were manufactured from semiconductor materials. Germanium and silicon were among the materials originally used, but silicon finally became predominant because of its ability to withstand higher temperatures and its relative ease of manufacture. A semiconductor is so named because it literally "semi-conducts." If the silicon is "doped" with certain "impurities" (elements other than pure silicon) in a chemical process at elevated temperatures, and then the proper electrical connections are made, the silicon will conduct electricity far easier in one direction than another. Further adjustments of the material and the outside connections will produce a wide range of electrical functions. All of this can be achieved from a solid block of cheap and widely available material with connections made by "bonding" gold wires to its surface. No vacuum processing and the delicate hermetic seals required with vacuum tubes are necessary. The processing of the silicon lends itself naturally to mass production. When transistors were introduced, chemists and physicists were added to electrical engineers at many companies to improve the performance of the transistors and to improve their ease of manufacture (and thus lower the cost of achieving a certain function).

After about a decade of working with transistors and their related circuitry, the next obvious (at least in retrospect) step was made. That step was the integrated circuit. The integrated circuit was a response to the problem that no matter how small you made transistors, you still had to connect them to each other and to other electronic components, and put them in a box to perform a specified electrical function. This was tedious (and thus expensive) handwork that did not lend itself easily to mass production. Also, it created a number of potential new failure points no matter how reliable the basic transistor and its related components happened to be. As is often the case, two men discovered a solution to this problem at nearly the same time.

Jack Kilby, a new engineering employee of the Texas Instruments company in Texas, was spending the summer vacation period of July 1958 relatively alone because he was not yet eligible for vacation pay. Kilby was studying the interconnection problem, when an idea occurred to him of how to build electronic components like capacitors and resistors in the same block of silicon used to make the transistor. He had a working model by September 1958, and in February 1959 Texas Instruments filed a patent application. Their so-called "Solid Circuit" was introduced to the world in March 1959.

At the newly formed Fairchild Semiconductor Company in California (formed in 1957 primarily by people who left the Shockley Semiconductor Company), solid-state physicist Bob Noyce took a slightly different approach in January 1959. Noyce concentrated on the interconnection of the transistor and the electronic components "grown" into a common block of silicon. In the spring of 1959 Fairchild announced its "unitary circuit," and wrote a careful, highly detailed patent application for the device in a way that (they hoped) would not infringe on the patent application that Texas Instruments had made in February 1959. This careful effort was rewarded with a patent on April 25, 1961, while the patent request from Kilby and Texas Instruments was still being analyzed.

Fairchild Semiconductor launched itself into the "integrated circuit" business with great success. Essentially an entire new industry was created, and with many companies expending many engineering hours over the next decade and into the 1970s, integrated circuits became routine. The basic approach was to chemically deposit large numbers of circuits on a properly prepared silicon "wafer," then — after a complicated series of high-temperature processing steps — simply "saw" the wafer apart into individual "chips" forming circuits already containing the number of transistors and circuit components necessary to perform a specific electrical function (or functions). Mass processing such as this made the chips nearly identical, thus highly reliable, and relatively cheap on a per-unit basis. Learning how to start the process using wafers of ever-increasing size eventually greatly increased the yield of useable chips from a single "run" through the ovens. Circuits of very high complexity were manufactured at relatively low prices, and the use of integrated circuits permeated both military and consumer electronics.

The next step in this tale of semiconductor manufacturing was the microprocessor. In 1968, Bob Noyce and Gordon Moore formed the Intel

Corporation. Both men left Fairchild Semiconductor to do so, but they really were the last of the key founders to leave as many of their previous associates had already left Fairchild (as rich men) after the East Coast ownership of the successful company became more onerous. It was this exodus from Fairchild by men who wanted to run their own businesses that was the basic foundation for what later became known as the "Silicon Valley." Intel was planning to concentrate on memory chips for the computer industry (primarily IBM) as semiconductor chips were just beginning to replace magnetic-core memories in computers. There was no thought of anything called the microprocessor at the time, and personal computers were just the dream of amateur computer "hackers."

In 1971, an Intel engineer named Ted Hoff developed a new approach to an electronic calculator program being built for a Japanese company called Busicom. Rather than utilizing a time-consuming process to build computer logic chips for the program, Hoff proposed a new way to design the device circuitry so that the chip to be used would actually contain enough equivalent transistors to act as a miniaturized general-purpose computer on its own. After some difficulty, the chip was built and turned out to be very useful for the program. However, reaction to Hoff's achievement at Intel was mixed. Intel was very busy working on memory chips and no one foresaw wide applications for the microprocessor.

It must be noted that the number of transistors on a single chip had been growing steadily for years. In 1965, while still at Fairchild, Intel co-founder Gordon Moore had taken note of this phenomenon and issued a paper forecasting steady growth in the number of transistors on a chip, specifying an "impossible" growth rate of a doubling nearly every year. The press dubbed this "Moore's Law" and the name stuck. The circuit and associated chip Hoff designed had 2,250 transistors per chip, a significant leap in transistors per chip, but not totally out of line with Moore's Law. Since 1971 the increase has been closer to a doubling every couple of years, still an amazing rate, and today Intel is talking about a billion transistors per chip.

When the Japanese calculator program was resolved, Intel introduced the microprocessor in November 1971 with a big advertisement announcing a "New Era in Integrated Electronics." Intel called it the 4004, and Gordon Moore said it was "one of the most revolutionary products in the history of mankind." Their statements eventually proved to be true, but it took some time for the microprocessor to find its way into new designs of electronic equipment.

Intel kept bringing out more and more powerful microprocessors as it improved its manufacturing processes, and by 1978 the Intel 8086 featured 29,000 transistors per chip. Other big semiconductor companies such as Texas Instruments and Motorola introduced their versions of a microprocessor, and the personal computer industry came almost literally out of nowhere in the mid–1970s, with Apple Computer taking the lead in the later 1970s. Motorola got its microprocessor chip into Apple's personal computers, but Intel caught the biggest fish when it beat out Texas Instruments to become the microprocessor used in IBM's entry into the personal computer market in 1981.

In an iterative way, microprocessor manufacturing techniques kept improving and personal computers and related equipment became more and more powerful and useful as designers learned to use the increasingly powerful microprocessors. Intel crossed the one-million-transistors-per-chip mark in 1989, and specific personal computer makers became less and less important — what mattered was whether the machine used an Intel microprocessor (and Microsoft software). Intel became the largest chipmaker in the world, and its sales and constant development of more complex microprocessors led the way.

BIBLIOGRAPHY

The Bibliography lists the key books consulted in writing this chronology. The field of communication is very large and complex, but books that cover well specific areas of the field are discussed in the paragraphs below.

A good overview of the development of wireless communication by Marconi and others and its transition into radio and television is presented in *Empire of the Air* by Tom Lewis. This book is a good start into understanding how electronic communication established its foothold in roughly the first half of the twentieth century.

The next step in communications after radio and television is well presented by Helen Gavaghan in *Something New Under the Sun*, a comprehensive history of the development of communication (and other) satellites in the 1950s and 1960s.

Jeff Hecht's *City of Light*, covers the development of fiber-optic communication systems. This book not only is an excellent history of fiber optics, it also provides useful general background about the way that telephone and related communication systems work and what factors are important in their proper functioning regardless of whether they are "conventional" systems, or satellite based, or fiber-optic based.

The development and evolution of the next major step in communications, the personal computer, is covered in two excellent books. The first is *Fire in the Valley* by Paul Freiberger and Michael Swaine. This book is not only a very good history of the development of the personal computer, but it chronicles the growth of what became known as the "Silicon Valley." As the history of the personal computer unfolds, the role that Microsoft and Intel played in the initial development, and how these companies finally became the main drivers of the personal computer industry, also become clear.

Continuing with the personal computer, *Blue Magic* by James Chposky and Ted Leonsis tells a story that is somewhat narrower in scope, but which tells the "other side" of the tale. This book focuses on mighty IBM and its decision to enter the personal computer market with its highly successful IBM PC in 1981. The story of how it happened and what took place afterwards confirms how Microsoft and Intel became the major pillars of the personal computer industry even when a company as large and powerful as IBM was involved.

Abbate, Janet. *Inventing the Internet.* Cambridge, Mass.: MIT Press, 2000.

Berners-Lee, Tim, with Mark Fischetti. *Weaving the Web: The Original Design and Ultimate Destiny of the World Wide Web.* New York: HarperCollins Publishers, Inc., 2000.

Bridgewater, William, and Seymour Kurtz, eds. *The Columbia Encyclopedia.* 3rd ed. New York: Columbia University Press, 1963.

Byers, Ann. *The Library of Satellites: Communications Satellites.* New York: Rosen Publishing Group, 2003.

Chposky, James, and Ted Leonsis. *Blue Magic: The People, Power, and Politics behind the IBM Personal Computer.* New York: Facts on File Publications, 1988.

Freiberger, Paul, and Michael Swaine. *Fire in the Valley: The Making of the Personal Computer.* 2nd ed. New York: McGraw-Hill, 2000.

Gavaghan, Helen. *Something New Under the Sun: Satellites and the Beginning of the Space Age.* New York: Copernicus/Springer-Verlag, 1998.

Gleick, James. *Isaac Newton.* New York: Pantheon Books, 2003.

Graham, Ian. *Technoworld: Satellites and Communications.* Austin, Texas: Steck-Vaughn Company, 2001.

Head, Sydney W., and Christopher H. Sterling. *Broadcasting in America: A Survey of Television, Radio, and New Technologies.* 4th ed. Boston: Houghton Mifflin Company, 1982.

Hecht, Jeff. *City of Light: The Story of Fiber Optics.* New York: Oxford University Press, 1999.

Heilemann, John. *Pride Before the Fall: The Trials of Bill Gates and the End of the Microsoft Era.* New York: HarperCollins Publishers, Inc., 2002.

Holland, Gini, and Amy Stone. *Inventors and Inventions: Telephones.* New York: Marshall Cavendish Corporation, 1996.

Irwin, Keith Gordon. *The Romance of Writing: From Egyptian Hieroglyphics to Modern Letters, Numbers, and Signs.* New York: Viking Press, 1956.

Jackson, Tim. *Inside Intel: Andy Grove and the Rise of the World's Most Powerful Chip Company.* New York: Penguin Group, 1997.

Kanter, Rosabeth Moss. *Evolve! Succeeding in the Digital Culture of Tomorrow.* Boston: Harvard Business School Press, 2001.

Lewis, Tom. *Empire of the Air: The Men Who Made Radio.* New York: HarperCollins Publishers, Inc., 1991.

Mattern, Joanne. *Telephones.* Berkeley Heights, N.J.: Enslow Publishers, Inc., 2002.

Maxwell, Fredric Alan. *Bad Boy Ballmer: The Man Who Rules Microsoft.* New York: HarperCollins Publishers, Inc., 2002.

McCullough, David. *John Adams.* New York: Simon & Schuster, 2001.

Quittner, Joshua, and Michelle Slatalla. *Speeding the Net: The Inside Story of Netscape and How It Challenged Microsoft.* New York: Atlantic Monthly Press, 1998.

Schwartz, Evan I. *The Last Lone Inventor: A Tale of Genius, Deceit, and the Birth of Television.* New York: HarperCollins Publishers, Inc., 2002.

Tiner, John Hudson. *100 Scientists Who Shaped World History.* San Mateo, California: Bluewood Books, 2000.

Wells, H. G. *The Outline of History: The Whole Story of Man.* Vols. 1 and 2. Garden City, N.Y.: Doubleday, 1971.

Wise, William. *The Story of Communication: From Scrolls to Satellites.* New York: Parents Magazine Press, 1970.

World Almanac and Book of Facts, 2004. New York: World Almanac Books, 2004.

Yenne, Bill, and Dr. Morton Grossner. *100 Inventions That Shaped World History.* San Mateo, CA: Bluewood Books, 1993.

INDEX